Paleo Slow Cooker Recipes

65 Fast, Easy and Delicious Primal Crock Pot Recipes to Feed Your Family

Andrea Huffington

Atlanta, Georgia USA

ISBN 978-1-49101-025-9

Copyright © 2012 Andrea Huffington

Readers' Feedback

"I've been on the Paleo diet six months now, and being able to use a slow cooker has made it definitely easier to stick with it. I recommend buying this book, it shows you exactly what to do."

★★★★★ Russel S. Dewitt – Texas

"This little ebook is just a gem for a busy mom like me, trying to balance work, family and health. Buy it!"

★★★★☆ Theresa C. Cali – Minneapolis

"when I come home from class and gym, my meal is there waiting for me. This makes being on the Paleo lifestyle so much easier. Andrea Huffington has made the whole process so simple, thank you."

★★★★☆ Austin Gurner - Australia

Thank you for downloading my book. Please REVIEW this book on Amazon. I need your feedback to make the next version better. Thank you so much!

A Few Words From the Author

If someone told you that all you had to do to save time when it comes to cooking was to take it slow, would you believe them? Well, the truth is that slow cooking does save you time, if not for any other reason for the simple fact that many of its recipes require up to ten hours to cook.

That doesn't sound quite right, does it? But it is right and by going through the pages of my book you'll find out how this actually works, what are the benefits of slow cooking and much more. Slow cooking is something that can be beneficial to you and your family in many ways since it can also be used to prepare special recipes that have to do with the Paleo diet, while if done correctly it can even add taste to your food.

However, when I set out to write this book I did not only want to talk about slow cooking. So in here you'll also find instructions of how to follow a special diet, as well as a list of substitute products that can help improve your health. If read my book you'll soon come to understand that sometimes things can be done easily and without much trouble.

TABLE OF CONTENTS

ONE LAST THING... 97

Disclaimer

While all attempts have been made to provide effective, verifiable information in this Book, neither the Author nor Publisher assumes any responsibility for errors, inaccuracies, or omissions. Any slights of people or organizations are unintentional.

This Book is not a source of medical information, and it should not be regarded as such. This publication is designed to provide accurate and authoritative information in regard to the subject matter covered. It is sold with the understanding that the publisher is not engaged in rendering a medical service. As with any medical advice, the reader is strongly encouraged to seek professional medical advice before taking action.

Slow Cooking Basics

If you've ever come home from a long day of work, only to be faced with the overwhelming prospect of making dinner from scratch, you already understand the benefits of a slow cooker. While the name makes it sound like something you wouldn't want to deal with at a time like this, it's actually one of the few kitchen appliances that will prevent this situation in the first place. In the story of how she started using her slow cooker, Hope, the writer of slowcookeradventures.com, tells of how she felt like she didn't have time to spend with her daughter after she picked her up from daycare, got home, and made dinner. Crock pot to the rescue!

So what is slow cooking? It's exactly like it sounds—cooking food slowly. Very slowly. In fact, many recipes call for 6, 8, or even 10 hours of cooking time. You may be asking yourself why you would ever want to spend that much time cooking, but the beauty of slow cooking is that you don't have to be there. You can set your slow cooker (also known as a crock pot) in the morning, throw in all of the ingredients before you go to work, and have a steaming, healthy dinner prepared when you get home. Whip up a side salad, and you have yourself a meal for your entire family with minimal evening preparation.

When you use a slow cooker for the first time, if you're like me, you'll worry about burning the dish. However, one of the best parts about slow cooking is that it's nearly impossible to mess up. You're working with low heat and a lot of liquid, which keeps the food from burning, adds moisture, and enhances the flavor. That's one of the reasons that you see a lot of comfort foods in crock pot recipe books: soups, chilis, roasts, and the like. But slow cooking is very versatile; you can make rice dishes, meatballs, even desserts in a slow cooker! If you can think of something that sounds impossible to make in a slow cooker, it's likely that someone has figured out a way.

In addition to the benefits mentioned above, there are several others that should be mentioned. For example, a crock pot is a great way to keep your food warm throughout the meal, in case someone wants seconds (and they likely will). It also uses less energy, reducing your bills and being better for the environment. And not only that, but using a slow cooker means that you don't have to use your oven, which helps keep your house cooler during the summer, and also opens up another cooking appliance for if you're working on multiple dishes (or making dessert at the same time).

Slow cooking techniques and tips

One of the most significant benefits of slow cooking is that it's remarkably easy. In fact, that's one of the main reasons that most people use it. However, there are a few things to keep in mind that will help you get the most out of your crock pot and the dishes you make with it; even though this might add a few steps to your recipes, it's totally worth it, because you can make a world of difference with just a bit of effort. Here are five tips for getting the most out of your slow cooker:

- Cook on low.

Most slow cookers have two settings: low and high. Sometimes you want to use the high setting to get food done more quickly. However, if at all possible, use the low setting, as your dishes will be more moist, and the meats will be more tender, than if you use high. And although it's always tough to burn things in a crock pot, it's even harder on the low setting.

- Know your crock pot.

More details on this are coming in the next section, but it needs to be mentioned here: know how your crock pot works. Not just when it comes to turning it on and setting the timer, but also if it tends to run hotter or cooler than average and if it takes a long time to heat up. If you know these things, you'll be able to alter your recipes to ensure that they work best with your slow cooker.

- Prepare your slow cooker for each dish.

Another way to ensure that burning is less likely is to correctly prepare your slow cooker before you add the ingredients. You can use an oil (like canola) spray, or you can line the crock pot with foil. I recommend the spray, but using foil definitely makes clean-up easier!

- Be careful with chicken.

This applies to any meat or poultry that you use, but especially with chicken: don't overcook it. Even though the crock pot is full of liquid, you can sometimes accidentally create tough and stringy meat. To prevent this, always cook chicken on low, and don't cook it for more than six hours (unless your cooker is very slow).

- Adapt recipes to your slow cooker.

Many crock pot recipes call for a specific size of slow cooker. Some people solve this problem by keeping multiple crock pots on hand, but you can also adapt your current one to work with the recipe you have. In order to do this, it's important to remember that slow cookers work best when they are between 1/2 and 3/4 full. So if you have a recipe for a 2-quart crock pot that you're adapting for a 4-quart one, you'll need more ingredients (possibly up to twice as much of each).

Getting to Know Your Slow Cooker Features and Settings

A crock pot is a pretty simple thing, but it's worth taking a little space here—and a little time on your part—to make sure that you fully understand how it works and how to best use it.

Anatomy of a Crock Pot

There are, basically, four parts to a crock pot. There's the base, which is the lowermost part of the whole thing, and it's usually made of metal, though it may have a plastic covering. The crock is the heavy ceramic piece that sits on top of the base, and into which you insert your ingredients. The controls are usually on the front of the base, and often include little more than a switch that has off, low, and high settings and a timer, though some have considerably more controls, while some only have a power switch. Finally, the slow cooker has a power cord that, obviously, needs to be plugged in for cooking.

How do I choose a high-quality and reliable crock pot?

Doing a little research to determine the best slow cooker for you will definitely pay off in the long run. It can also be beneficial to collect a few recipes that you plan on trying before you buy a slow cooker so that you know what you'll need. For example, some recipes are best made in a 4-quart crock, while others work better in a 6-quart one. This also depends on the size of the meals you want to make; if you have a large family, a bigger one will be better. If you're just cooking for one or two people, however, you can probably get away with a smaller one.

There are other differences between crock pots that also make a difference in which one you want to buy, like the controls that it offers. Obviously, a timer is beneficial. But do you want one that you can also *start* on a timer? This can be nice if you have a recipe that calls for 6 hours of cooking when you work an 8-hour day. Some crock pots have lids that can be secured as well, which is nice if you're transporting the crock full of food (to a potluck, say). There are many different features that you can have on your slow cooker—just remember that the more features it has, the more expensive it will be. Fortunately, slow cookers are generally quite reasonably priced.

When it comes to reliability, your best bet is to buy a crock pot from a reputable brand. These are the same as with most other kitchen appliances, like GE, KitchenAid, and Cuisinart. The Crock-Pot brand is also of high quality. Fortunately, crockpots have no moving parts, so they don't undergo a lot of wear, and should last a long time.

Testing your crockpot

The team at America's Test Kitchen recommend this procedure for determining whether your slow cooker runs hotter or cooler than average: add four quarts of room-temperature water to your cooker, then turn it on for four hours. After the four hours are complete, use an instant-read thermometer to measure the temperature of the water. If it's higher or lower than 195¬¬–205 degrees, you may have to make some adjustments in your cooking time.

Paleo Slow Cooking Made Easy

One of the best things about slow cooking is that you can make almost anything you want. If you put 'slow cooker' and the name of a food that you like into a search engine, you're bound to get a lot of results. This is especially nice if you're following the Paleo diet, because it can be somewhat limiting at times. The health benefits are worth it, though, so finding ways to easily prepare your meals is crucial.

What is the Paleo diet?

'Paleo' is short for 'Paleolithic', a term that describes the period of time around 10,000 years ago. The diet has this name because it only includes foods that were around during this time period. To make a long, scientific story short, the human body hasn't evolved to process foods that have come about more recently than this, which includes gluten-based grains, processed foods, and most dairy products. People following the Paleo diet eat primarily lean meats, fruits and vegetables, roots, and nuts, and many of them completely cut out gluten (which is derived from wheat). Obviously, these are only the basics, but there is a wealth of information available for free online.

If you're on the Paleo diet, you have a large arsenal of recipes available to you, many of which include several servings of the key foods in the diet, like lean meat and vegetables, which are the main ingredients of most crock pot recipes. Some foods don't take well to long hours of cooking, but these do, and that's a huge benefit to anyone trying to stick to the Paleo diet, especially if you find it difficult (or just don't want) to spend the time it takes to cook a healthy, Paleo-compliant meal after work.

And while there are loads of recipes that you can use, it's always good to remember that if you're really rushed, you can just throw a bunch of things in the crock pot, add some water and a little seasoning, and let it go all day. You may not come home to something that's worthy of a 5-star restaurant, but it's certainly better than having to start from scratch after a really long day of work or running the kids around to their various weekend events.

Can a vegetarian be Paleo?

As a vegetarian, getting enough protein is crucial, and it's usually provided by soy and other beans. Can you get enough protein without these? The short answer is yes. It is possible, though it may require a few changes to the generally accepted principles of the diet. For example, Matt Frazier of No Meat Athlete suggests soaking dry beans before cooking them, thereby removing many of the enzyme inhibitors that are naturally present in them (which he says is the main problem with beans in the first place, instead of simply the fact that Paleolithic humans didn't eat them). It's also possible to ignore or modify the restriction on grain-like seeds, including quinoa, amaranth, and buckwheat. You're still not eating grains, but you're adding some less-detrimental seeds to your diet. And, of course, you can always eat eggs, which contain a lot of protein.

As you can see, the Paleo diet can be modified to work with a vegetarian diet. It's good to remember that a diet doesn't have to be an all-or-nothing endeavor. If all of the rules of a specific diet don't work with your lifestyle, you can modify a few of them and still get most of the benefits of the diet. This is true of any diet, including Paleo. It's important to remember that the Paleo diet doesn't recommend eating the foods that it does just because it seems like a good idea, but because they contribute to a proper pH in the body, reduce inflammation, and are easily processed. If you keep these ideas in mind while choosing your foods, you'll be staying true to the Paleo lifestyle, even if you don't obey every single rule to the letter.

Slow cooking tips for a Paleo gluten-free diet

Using a slow cooker is a great way to prepare a lot of the foods that are often found in gluten-free Paleo diets. It's easy to get stuck in a rut of eating salad after salad, with an omelet thrown in every once in a while, but by adding slow cooker recipes to your cookbook, you'll have a large variety of easily prepared foods at your disposal. And not only are they easy to prepare, but they're also healthy and delicious—what more could you ask for?

In order to adapt your gluten-free diet to the Paleo rules, you'll have to make a lot of substitutions. The standard Western diet is full of gluten, not only from bread, but also from related products, like pasta, pizza crust, and many sauces and soups. These are things that most people eat every day (and in some cases, several times a day). Going gluten-free isn't easy, but combining it with the Paleo diet can help. Many blogs and other sites have lists of really great substitutions for Paleo dieters that can also be very beneficial to those on gluten-free diets. For example, a lot of recipes replace pasta with spaghetti squash. Bread can be made out of things other than wheat flour, and even pancakes and cookies have Paleo versions. Dairy milk can be replaced with coconut milk, and there are quite a few products derived from nuts that can replace cheese. Once you've committed to being Paleo and gluten-free, it's pretty amazing what you can come up with.

How can I add flavor to my Paleo dishes?

One of the most important things in making Paleo-compliant meals—especially if you have kids—is making sure that they taste good. Really, no matter how healthy something is, if it's not tasty, you're not going to want to eat it. And your kids certainly won't, either. By using the following tips on making your slow cooker dishes as flavorful as possible, you can keep yourself from facing bland food day after day.

1. Brown meat before adding it to the crock pot.

By using high heat to brown the meat before putting it in with the rest of the ingredients, you seal in the juices that will make it both juicy and flavorful, You can also toss it in an herb and almond flour batter before browning it, which will give it a bit of added crispness.

2. Look for recipes with splashes of fruit or juice.

I recently used a recipe for meatballs that included black currants, and these really helped add a bit of sweetness to the whole dish. Sometimes a sliced apple, a splash of apple juice or a bit of lime juice added at the end of the cooking time can make a huge difference in giving a dish a little extra kick.

3. Use your crockpot as a smoker.

This one requires a bit of bravery, but can infuse some of the flavor of grilling into your crockpot! Stephanie O'Dea has a great article on how to do this (http://crockpot365.blogspot.co.uk/2008/08/you-can-use-your-crockpot-as-smoker.html), but here's the short version: soak 1-2 cups of mesquite wood chips in water for at least 30 minutes, then drain. Wrap the chips in parchment paper, and poke tiny holes in the top of the paper packet that you've created. Rub your chosen meat with a spice rub, and then put it in on top of the mesquite packet. Cover with water, and cook for 8–10 hours. Voila!

4. Add herbs at the end of the cooking time.

This is an easy and important one; because soaking herbs can reduce some of the flavor, throw them in at the end of the recipe, instead of at the beginning, and they'll add even more punch to your dish.

5. Add soy sauce to enhance the flavors of meat.

Although there are a lot of different things that you can add to enhance the flavors of specific foods, soy sauce is a good general one to keep on hand, especially if you're cooking red meat, like beef or venison. However, soy sauce contains soy and sometimes wheat thus it's not allowed in a Paleo diet. You can buy Paleo soy sauce from Amazon (brand: Coconut Secret) or you could make your own. I've included a couple of Paleo homemade say sauce in my recipe list below.

Losing Weight in 30 Days with a Slow Cooker

Though there are many ways to effectively lose weight, I find that a slow cooker is a fantastic way to do it, especially if you're just getting started. Why is it so helpful? First, because having dinner ready when you get home means that you'll be less likely to order takeout on the way home (which, I know, can be awfully tempting when you have to feed several children). Knowing that you have a tasty and healthy meal waiting for you also goes a long way to curb some of your snacking impulses, as you know you won't have to wait for an hour or two while you're preparing dinner. Slow cooker recipes are often very filling soups, stews, and chilis, too. All of these combine to mean that you're more likely to consume the proper number of calories in a day, as well as stick to foods that are high in nutrients.

Second, slow cooker meals are easy to portion out. If you're counting calories, you can add up the total for the whole dish and divide it by however many servings you've made. Then simply weigh the whole thing on a kitchen scale and portion out servings. After you've eaten dinner, you can pack up the leftovers so you have lunch for the next day, and it's already been counted and portioned. What could be easier?

By combining healthy slow cooking with good eating practices throughout the day and exercising several times a week, losing weight in 30 days is no problem. And the more meals you use the slow cooker for, the easier this becomes. If you cook three dinners in a week in a crock pot, that's three dinners and three lunches that you've taken care of, which means you don't have to think about finding a healthy option at work or at home for six meals. Not bad for one of the easiest ways to prepare a meal!

Smart eating: healthy substitutions

When you're starting a diet, no matter if it's Paleo, Primal, macrobiotic, or anything else, one of the best ways to start cutting calories is by substituting allowable items for disallowed ones. This is especially important with the Paleo diet, as many of the things that are prohibited by the diet are central to cooking and baking, and finding new recipes for everything would take a long time (and your kids wouldn't be very happy if you told them that they can no longer have their favorite dish because it's not gluten-free). It's impossible to list all of the substitutions that you could possibly make, so I'll stick to the basics here. If you need more help, you can easily find more information on substitutions by searching for 'Paleo substitutes' or 'gluten-free substitutions' online.

Although there are a lot of things are difficult to go without, a lot of people find that it's hardest giving up their main sources of carbohydrates. The Western diet has a lot of grains of various kinds, and in various forms, so it can be very beneficial to find good substitutes for these. For example, if you're craving pasta, you can replace it with spaghetti squash, or julienne-sliced zucchini or carrots. If you want rice, a popular substitute is riced cauliflower. If you want something to replace the sauce you usually use with pasta or rice, you can use canned pumpkin or butternut squash. Mashed potatoes can be replaced by mashed turnips or, depending on who you ask, mashed sweet potatoes. You can also use malanga or yucca.

Another category of foods that is hard to give up, but can easily be replaced, are dairy products. For example, you can almost always replace any milk in your recipe with almond or hazelnut milk. Instead of butter, you can use ghee (a form of clarified butter). It's more difficult to replace cheeses, but there are vegan and dairy-free options available; it's also possible to make replacements using coconut, but some people find this to be too different from cheese to be an acceptable substitute.

Sweets can also be replaced; honey and stevia can be used in place of sugar, and cacao can stand in for chocolate in a pinch (though it does come from a legume, and some people consider this a violation of the Paleo rules). And if you're like me and crave ice cream on a regular basis, you can get some coconut ice cream, which is pretty easy to find, and surprisingly good.

65 Delicious & Easy Slow Cooker Recipes to Satisfy Your Craving

BREAKFAST

1. Slow Cooked Apple Breakfast Cobbler

Servings: 4
Preparation time: 10 minutes
Cook time: 3 hours on HIGH or 6 hours on LOW
Ready in: 3 hours and 10 minutes

Nutrition Facts		
Serving Size 341 g		
Amount Per Serving		
Calories 280		Calories from Fat 64
		% Daily Value*
Total Fat 7.2g		**11%**
Saturated Fat 5.9g		**30%**
Trans Fat 0.0g		
Cholesterol 0mg		**0%**
Sodium 81mg		**3%**
Total Carbohydrates 55.8g		**19%**
Dietary Fiber 9.2g		**37%**
Sugars 40.2g		
Protein 1.1g		
Vitamin A 4%	•	Vitamin C 23%
Calcium 8%	•	Iron 13%
Nutrition Grade C		
* Based on a 2000 calorie diet		

Ingredients
- 6 apples, peeled, cored and thinly sliced
- 1 tablespoon coconut oil

- 1/2 cup full-fat coconut milk (see Recipe No. 63), or almond milk
- 1/2 cup shredded unsweetened Coconut
- 1/2 cup raisins (or dried cranberries)
- 1 tablespoon cinnamon
- 1/2 teaspoon ground ginger
- dash of sea salt
- 1 tablespoon pure vanilla extract

Directions

Grease crockpot with coconut oil. Mix all ingredients in a 3-quart crockpot. Cook on low for 6 hours, high for 3 hours, or overnight. Serve topped with raw nuts and shredded coconut.

2. Crockpot Veggies and Meat Breakfast Pie

Servings: 4-6
Preparation time: 10 minutes
Cook time: 6-8 hours on LOW
Ready in: 6 hours and 10 minutes

Nutrition Facts

Serving Size 220 g

Amount Per Serving

Calories 269	Calories from Fat 156

% Daily Value*

Total Fat 17.3g	**27%**
Saturated Fat 1.8g	**9%**
Trans Fat 0.0g	
Cholesterol 218mg	**73%**
Sodium 150mg	**6%**
Total Carbohydrates 7.6g	**3%**
Dietary Fiber 1.9g	**7%**
Sugars 3.7g	
Protein 21.4g	

Vitamin A 130%	•	Vitamin C 16%
Calcium 5%	•	Iron 8%

Nutrition Grade B

* Based on a 2000 calorie diet

Ingredients
- 8 eggs, whisked
- 2 cups carrots, diced

- 1 1/2 cups zucchini, diced
- 1pound lean ground pork
- 1 onion, diced
- 1 tablespoon garlic powder
- 2 teaspoons dried basil
- 1 teaspoon dried parsley flakes
- sea salt and pepper, to taste

Directions

Grease a 4-quart crockpot with coconut oil. Combine all ingredients to the crockpot; mix well. Cook on low for 6-8 hours. Slice and serve warm.

3. Winter Breakfast Apple Peach Sauce with Almonds

Servings: 12
Preparation time: 10 minutes
Cook time: 3 hours on HIGH or 6 hours on LOW
Ready in: 3 hours and 10 minutes

Nutrition Facts

Serving Size 185 g

Amount Per Serving

Calories 94	Calories from Fat 1

% Daily Value*

Total Fat 0.1g	0%
Trans Fat 0.0g	
Cholesterol 0mg	0%
Sodium 2mg	0%
Total Carbohydrates 24.6g	8%
Dietary Fiber 4.4g	18%
Sugars 18.6g	
Protein 0.3g	

Vitamin A 4%	•	Vitamin C 15%
Calcium 2%	•	Iron 2%

Nutrition Grade A-
* Based on a 2000 calorie diet

Ingredients
- 10 Macintosh or Granny Smith apples, peeled, cored and chopped
- 4 fresh peaches, peeled, pitted and chopped
- 1 tablespoon ground cinnamon
- 1/2 teaspoon pure vanilla extract
- 1 pinch of unrefined brown sugar

Directions

- Place fruits in a 4-quart slow cooker. Sprinkle with cinnamon and vanilla; toss gently.
- Cover and cook for 3 hours on High, or 6 hours on Low. Serve with toasted almonds.

4. Crock Pot Blueberry Quinoa Porridge

Servings: 3-4

Preparation time: 10 minutes

Cook time: 9 hours on WARM

Ready in: 9 hours and 10 minutes

Nutrition Facts

Serving Size 300 g

Amount Per Serving

Calories 239   Calories from Fat 34

% **Daily Value***

Total Fat 3.7g	**6%**
Trans Fat 0.0g	
Cholesterol 0mg	**0%**
Sodium 9mg	**0%**
Total Carbohydrates 47.2g	**16%**
Dietary Fiber 4.3g	**17%**
Sugars 19.5g	
Protein 6.1g	

Vitamin A 1%   •   Vitamin C 4%

Calcium 3%   •   Iron 12%

Nutrition Grade B

* Based on a 2000 calorie diet

Ingredients

- 1-1/2 cups of quinoa, rinsed
- 3-1/2 cups water
- 1/4 teaspoon vanilla extract
- 3/4 cup applesauce
- 1 teaspoon cinnamon
- 3 tablespoon raw honey
- 1/2 cup blueberries
- 1 tablespoon toasted pecans, chopped

Directions

Combine all ingredients in a 4-quart slow cooker. Cook for 9 hours on warm.

5. Crock Pot Paleo Bananas Foster with Walnuts

Servings: 4

Preparation time: 15 minutes

Cook time: 2 hours on LOW

Ready in: 2 hours 15 minutes

Nutrition Facts

Serving Size 184 g

Amount Per Serving

Calories 414　　　　　Calories from Fat 141

% Daily Value*

Total Fat 15.7g	**24%**
Saturated Fat 2.7g	**14%**
Trans Fat 0.0g	
Cholesterol 0mg	**0%**
Sodium 13mg	**1%**
Total Carbohydrates 67.2g	**22%**
Dietary Fiber 4.8g	**19%**
Sugars 50.1g	
Protein 6.8g	

Vitamin A 2%	•	Vitamin C 18%
Calcium 9%	•	Iron 12%

Nutrition Grade C+

* Based on a 2000 calorie diet

Ingredients

- 4 bananas, peeled and sliced 1/2 inch thick
- 4 tablespoons almond butter
- 1 cup packed unrefined brown sugar
- 1 teaspoon vanilla extract
- 1/2 teaspoon ground cinnamon
- 1/4 cup walnuts, chopped
- 1/4 cup shredded coconut

Directions

- Combine sugar, butter, cinnamon, and vanilla in a 3-quart slow cooker. Add the banana slices to the butter mixture and toss to coat.

- Cover and set the slow cooker to low. Cook for 2 hours. Serve topped with walnuts and shredded coconut.

6. Crockpot Beef Meatballs

Servings: 7

Preparation time: 20 minutes

Cook time: 8 hours on LOW

Ready in: 8 hours 20 minutes

Nutrition Facts

Serving Size 280 g

Amount Per Serving

Calories 356   Calories from Fat 164

	% Daily Value*
Total Fat 18.2g	**28%**
Saturated Fat 6.0g	**30%**
Trans Fat 0.0g	
Cholesterol 156mg	**52%**
Sodium 199mg	**8%**
Total Carbohydrates 15.5g	**5%**
Dietary Fiber 3.9g	**15%**
Sugars 8.3g	
Protein 32.8g	

Vitamin A 43%	•	Vitamin C 36%
Calcium 8%	•	Iron 32%

Nutrition Grade B-

* Based on a 2000 calorie diet

Ingredients
- 2 pounds grass-fed ground beef
- 1/2 cup carrots, chopped
- 1 large onion, chopped
- 1/2 cup celery, chopped
- 3 eggs
- 1/2 cup almond meal
- 1 teaspoon dried oregano
- 3 cloves garlic, minced
- 1/8 teaspoon ground black pepper
- 1 teaspoon raw honey
- 2 cups diced tomatoes
- 1 cup organic tomato paste
- 1/2 cup fresh basil leaves, chopped

22

- 5 garlic cloves, coarsely chopped
- 1/8 teaspoon sea salt
- 1 pinch of black pepper

Directions
- Combine first 10 ingredients in a large bowl. Roll mixture into large meatballs and place into the crockpot. In a medium bowl, mix the diced tomatoes, tomato paste, basil, garlic, salt, and pepper.
- Pour the tomato sauce over the meatballs. Cook on Low for 8 hours or all day.

7. Classic Crock Pot Baked Apples

Servings: 6
Serving size: 1 baked apple
Preparation time: 10 minutes
Cook time: 4 hours on LOW
Ready in: 4 hours and 10 minutes

Nutrition Facts

Serving Size 214 g

Amount Per Serving

Calories 219　　　　　　Calories from Fat 69

% Daily Value*

Total Fat 7.7g	**12%**
Trans Fat 0.0g	
Cholesterol 0mg	**0%**
Sodium 5mg	**0%**
Total Carbohydrates 36.7g	**12%**
Dietary Fiber 6.1g	**25%**
Sugars 27.4g	
Protein 3.2g	

Vitamin A 2%	•	Vitamin C 16%
Calcium 4%	•	Iron 5%

Nutrition Grade B+

* Based on a 2000 calorie diet

Ingredients
- 6 apples, cored, peeled off a little around the top
- 1/2 cup dried cranberries (or raisins)
- 1/3 cup unrefined brown sugar
- 1 tablespoon organic almond butter
- 1 tablespoon cinnamon

- 1 tablespoon vanilla extract
- 1/2 cup walnuts, chopped (or pecans)

Directions
- Place apples into a 3-quart slow cooker. Combine dried cranberries, sugar, cinnamon, and vanilla in a small bowl.
- Spoon mixture into apples and top with almond butter. Cook on Low for 4 hours.

8. Slow Cooker Cocktail Smokies

Servings: 16
Preparation time: 50 minutes
Cook time: 2-3 hours on HIGH
Ready in: 2 hours and 50 minutes

Nutrition Facts

Serving Size 92 g

Amount Per Serving

Calories 139	Calories from Fat 55

	% Daily Value*
Total Fat 6.2g	**9%**
Saturated Fat 2.5g	**13%**
Trans Fat 0.0g	
Cholesterol 51mg	**17%**
Sodium 749mg	**31%**
Total Carbohydrates 12.8g	**4%**
Sugars 9.7g	
Protein 11.2g	

Vitamin A 3%	•	Vitamin C 4%	
Calcium 3%	•	Iron 7%	

Nutrition Grade D+

* Based on a 2000 calorie diet

Ingredients
- 2 (16 ounce) packages organic mini sausage links (recommended: Pork Kielbasa, Applegate Farms)
- 1 cup organic cranberry sauce
- 1/2 cup onion, chopped
- 1 1/2 cup Paleo barbecue sauce (see Recipe No. 64)
- 1/4 cup unrefined brown sugar

Directions

Stir together all the ingredients in a 4-quart slow cooker. Cook on High for 2 to 3 hours.

9. Super-Fast Crockpot Turkey Meatloaf

Servings: 5

Preparation time: 20 minutes

Cook time: 4 hours on HIGH or 6-8 hours on LOW

Ready in: 4 hours and 20 minutes

Nutrition Facts

Serving Size 268 g

Amount Per Serving

Calories 321	Calories from Fat 138
	% Daily Value*
Total Fat 15.3g	**24%**
Saturated Fat 4.6g	**23%**
Trans Fat 0.0g	
Cholesterol 194mg	**65%**
Sodium 317mg	**13%**
Total Carbohydrates 8.2g	**3%**
Dietary Fiber 2.8g	**11%**
Sugars 3.1g	
Protein 39.3g	

Vitamin A 98%	•	Vitamin C 12%
Calcium 8%	•	Iron 27%

Nutrition Grade B-

* Based on a 2000 calorie diet

Ingredients

Meatloaf:

- 2 pounds lean ground turkey
- 1 cup carrots, shredded
- 2 eggs, beaten
- 1/2 of a small white onion, diced
- 4 green onions, chopped
- 2 stacks of celery, chopped
- 2 teaspoons dried oregano
- 1 teaspoon black pepper
- 1 teaspoon thyme
- 2 teaspoon smoked paprika
- 2 teaspoon garlic powder

Sauce:

- 1/4 cup of tomato sauce
- 2 tablespoons Dijon mustard
- 2 teaspoon smoked paprika
- 2 teaspoon garlic powder
- 1 teaspoon apple cider vinegar

Directions

- Mix all the meatloaf ingredients in a large bowl. Combine well using your hands, and then form into a loaf.
- Place loaf in a 5-quart crockpot and pat lightly into the bottom. Mix the tomato sauce ingredients and spread over the top of the loaf.
- Cook on High for 4 hours, or 6-8 hours on Low.

10. Slow Cooked Fruity Squash

Servings: 10
Preparation time: 10 minutes
Cook time: 4 hours on HIGH
Ready in: 4 hours and 10 minutes

Nutrition Facts

Serving Size 220 g

Amount Per Serving

Calories 115　　　　　　　　　Calories from Fat 2

	% Daily Value*
Total Fat 0.2g	0%
Trans Fat 0.0g	
Cholesterol 0mg	0%
Sodium 7mg	0%
Total Carbohydrates 30.1g	10%
Dietary Fiber 5.2g	21%
Sugars 13.5g	
Protein 1.4g	

Vitamin A 290%	•	Vitamin C 55%
Calcium 8%	•	Iron 6%

Nutrition Grade A
* Based on a 2000 calorie diet

Ingredients

- 1 (3 pound) butternut squash, peeled, seeded, and cubed
- 4 apples, peeled, cored and chopped
- 3/4 cup dried cranberries

- 1 tablespoon ground cinnamon
- 1 teaspoon ground nutmeg
- 1 1/2 tablespoon raw honey (or maple syrup)

Directions
- Mix all ingredients together in a 6-quart slow cooker; toss to coat.
- Cook on high for 4 hours, until cooked through; stirring occasionally.

11. Slow-cooked Apples with Pumpkin Butter

Servings: 3
Serving size: 2 apple slices with 1/2 cup of pumpkin butter
Preparation time: 10 minutes
Cook time: 3 hours on HIGH or 6 hours on LOW
Ready in: 3 hours and 10 minutes

Nutrition Facts

Serving Size 465 g

Amount Per Serving

Calories 399 — Calories from Fat 157

	% Daily Value*
Total Fat 17.5g	**27%**
Saturated Fat 9.1g	**46%**
Trans Fat 0.0g	
Cholesterol 0mg	**0%**
Sodium 12mg	**1%**
Total Carbohydrates 59.8g	**20%**
Dietary Fiber 12.7g	**51%**
Sugars 41.7g	
Protein 4.7g	

Vitamin A 131%	•	Vitamin C 33%
Calcium 8%	•	Iron 13%

Nutrition Grade C

* Based on a 2000 calorie diet

Ingredients
- 6 apples, cored, peeled and sliced into wedges
- 1/2 cup organic pumpkin puree
- 1/2 cup full-fat coconut milk (see Recipe No. 63), or almond milk
- 1/2 cup almonds, chopped
- 1 tablespoon pure vanilla extract

- 1 tablespoon natural pumpkin pie spice

Directions
- Place the apples in the bottom of a 3-quart slow cooker.
- Mix together the pumpkin, coconut milk, almonds, vanilla, and pumpkin pie spice in a medium bowl. Pour mixture over apples in the slow cooker.
- Cook covered for 3 hours on High, or 6 hours on Low.

12. Crock Pot Carrot Cake

Servings: 16
Preparation time: 10 minutes
Cook time: 6 hours on LOW
Ready in: 6 hours 10 minutes

Nutrition Facts

Serving Size 240 g

Amount Per Serving

Calories 182 　　　Calories from Fat 90

	% Daily Value*
Total Fat 10.0g	**15%**
Trans Fat 0.0g	
Cholesterol 0mg	**0%**
Sodium 28mg	**1%**
Total Carbohydrates 24.9g	**8%**
Dietary Fiber 6.3g	**25%**
Sugars 16.5g	
Protein 4.1g	

Vitamin A 29%	•	Vitamin C 2%
Calcium 5%	•	Iron 7%

Nutrition Grade B

* Based on a 2000 calorie diet

Ingredients
- 10 cups water
- 3 cups unsweetened applesauce
- 2 cups flax meal
- 1 1/4 cup carrots, shredded
- 1 cup pecans, chopped
- 1 cup raisins
- 1/3 cup raw honey

- 2 tablespoons ground cinnamon
- 1 tablespoon pumpkin pie spice
- 1 pinch of sea salt

Directions

Combine all ingredients in a 7-quart slow cooker; mix well. Cook covered on Low for 6 hours.

13. Crock Pot Apple Carrot Ginger Soup

Servings: 4

Serving size: 1 cup

Preparation time: 10 minutes

Cook time: 4 hours on HIGH or 6 hours on LOW and 10 minutes

Ready in: 4 hours and 20 minutes

Nutrition Facts

Serving Size 172 g

Amount Per Serving

Calories 103   Calories from Fat 54

	% Daily Value*
Total Fat 6.0g	9%
Saturated Fat 4.3g	21%
Trans Fat 0.0g	
Cholesterol 0mg	0%
Sodium 31mg	1%
Total Carbohydrates 11.2g	4%
Dietary Fiber 2.3g	9%
Sugars 5.9g	
Protein 0.6g	

Vitamin A 116%	•	Vitamin C 10%
Calcium 2%	•	Iron 2%

Nutrition Grade B-

* Based on a 2000 calorie diet

Ingredients
- 1 teaspoon olive oil
- 1/2 cup onion, chopped
- 1 small thumb-size ginger, diced
- 1 1/4 cups carrots, diced
- 1 1/4 cups apples, diced
- 1 1/2 cups full fat coconut milk (see Recipe No. 63)
- sea salt and pepper

- 1/2 teaspoon cumin
- cayenne pepper (optional)
- scallions, chopped (optional)

Directions
- Mix together all ingredients except for the coconut milk in a 4-quart crockpot.
- Cook covered for 4 hours on High, or 6 hours on Low. Using a handheld blender, process mixture until smooth. Add the coconut milk into the soup and blend well.
- Ladle into bowls and garnish soup with cayenne pepper and chopped scallions.

14. Slow Cooked Banana Almond Bread

Servings: 6
Preparation time: 15 minutes
Cook time: 2-3 hours on HIGH
Ready in: 2 hours and 15 minutes

Nutrition Facts

Serving Size 207 g

Amount Per Serving

Calories 630   Calories from Fat 410

	% Daily Value*
Total Fat 45.5g	**70%**
Saturated Fat 23.1g	**116%**
Trans Fat 0.0g	
Cholesterol 55mg	**18%**
Sodium 568mg	**24%**
Total Carbohydrates 51.1g	**17%**
Dietary Fiber 10.0g	**40%**
Sugars 32.9g	
Protein 13.0g	

Vitamin A 2%	•	Vitamin C 11%
Calcium 13%	•	Iron 64%

Nutrition Grade D+

* Based on a 2000 calorie diet

Ingredients
- 1 cup ripe banana, mashed
- 1/2 cup almonds, chopped
- 1/2 cup almond butter (or coconut butter)

- 3/4 cup unrefined brown sugar
- 2 cups almond flour
- 1 teaspoon baking soda
- 1 teaspoon sea salt
- 2 eggs
- 2 1/2 tablespoons almond milk (or coconut milk)
- 1/4 teaspoon cinnamon
- 1/2 cup raisins
- 1 teaspoon pure vanilla extract
- Coconut oil for greasing

Directions

- In a medium bowl, combine the almond flour, baking soda, and salt. In another bowl, mix together the almond butter, sugar, and almonds.
- Add eggs, milk, vanilla, cinnamon, and the flour mixture; mix well. Stir in the mashed bananas and raisins until well blended.
- Grease an 8.5x4.5 inch loaf pan with coconut oil.
- Pour the batter into the pan and cover it with several paper towels. Place the pan inside 6-quart oval slow cooker. Place lid on slow cooker and bake on high for 2-3 hours.

15. Slow Cooker Chicken-Mushroom Soup

Servings: 4
Serving size: 1 medium bowl
Preparation time: 10 minutes
Cook time: 3-4 hours on HIGH or 6-8 hours on LOW and 10 minutes
Ready in: 3 hours and 20 minutes

Nutrition Facts

Serving Size 599 g

Amount Per Serving

Calories 363   Calories from Fat 105

                                                  % Daily Value*

Total Fat 11.7g	**18%**
Saturated Fat 1.9g	**10%**
Trans Fat 0.0g	
Cholesterol 129mg	**43%**
Sodium 1494mg	**62%**
Total Carbohydrates 8.7g	**3%**
Dietary Fiber 2.4g	**9%**
Sugars 3.7g	
Protein 55.3g	

Vitamin A 6%	•	Vitamin C 9%
Calcium 8%	•	Iron 18%

Nutrition Grade A-

* Based on a 2000 calorie diet

Ingredients

- 4 cups organic chicken broth
- 1 cup water
- 1 medium onion, chopped
- 3 cloves garlic, minced
- 1 tablespoon olive oil
- 8 ounces baby portabella mushrooms, sliced
- 4 cups lean chicken meat, cut in cubes
- 1 tablespoon Dijon mustard
- 2 teaspoons dried parsley
- 1 large rib celery, diced
- 1 tablespoon full-fat coconut milk (see Recipe No. 63)
- 1/8 teaspoon Sea salt
- 1/8 teaspoon pepper

Directions

- Place a skillet over medium heat. Once hot, pour the olive oil. Add the chicken cubes and cook until tender. Remove from skillet and set aside.
- On the same skillet, stir in the garlic and sauté until golden brown. Add the garlic and cook for another minute. Place the cooked chicken and sautéed onion and garlic into the slow cooker.

- Add the mushrooms, mustard, parsley, celery, salt and pepper; toss to coat. Pour the chicken broth, water, and coconut milk; stir well to combine.
- Cover and cook on High for 3-4 hours, or 6-8 hours on Low.

16. Crockpot Pumpkin Bread

Servings: 4
Preparation time: 10 minutes
Cook time: 3-3 ½ hours on HIGH
Ready in: 3 hours and 10 minutes

Nutrition Facts

Serving Size 230 g

Amount Per Serving

Calories 759	Calories from Fat 408

	% Daily Value*
Total Fat 45.3g	**70%**
Saturated Fat 31.1g	**156%**
Trans Fat 0.0g	
Cholesterol 82mg	**27%**
Sodium 796mg	**33%**
Total Carbohydrates 84.0g	**28%**
Dietary Fiber 18.3g	**73%**
Sugars 58.2g	
Protein 10.8g	

Vitamin A 193%	•	Vitamin C 5%
Calcium 6%	•	Iron 180%

Nutrition Grade C+

* Based on a 2000 calorie diet

Ingredients
- 1/2 cup coconut oil, with extra for greasing
- 1/2 cup raw honey
- 1/2 cup unrefined brown sugar
- 2 eggs, beaten
- 1 cup organic pumpkin puree
- 1 1/2 cup coconut flour, sifted
- 3/4 teaspoon sea salt
- 1 teaspoon pumpkin pie spice
- 1 teaspoon baking soda
- 1/2 cup pecans, chopped

Directions

- In a large bowl, combine the coconut oil, honey, and brown sugar. Stir in the beaten eggs and pumpkin puree.
- Add the remaining ingredients and blend well.
- Grease an 8.5x4.5 inch loaf pan with coconut oil. Pour batter into the loaf pan and place pan in a 5-6 quart oval crock pot.
- Cover top of pan with paper towels. Cover the crock pot and bake bread on high for 3 - 3 1/2 hours.

LUNCH

17. Crock Pot Pork Loin in Fruit Sauce

Servings: 8
Preparation time: 10 minutes
Cook time: 5-6 hours on LOW
Ready in: 5 hours and 10 minutes

Nutrition Facts

Serving Size 245 g

Amount Per Serving	
Calories 281	Calories from Fat 45
	% Daily Value*
Total Fat 4.9g	**8%**
Saturated Fat 2.1g	**11%**
Trans Fat 0.0g	
Cholesterol 83mg	**28%**
Sodium 161mg	**7%**
Total Carbohydrates 27.0g	**9%**
Dietary Fiber 1.5g	**6%**
Sugars 4.2g	
Protein 30.4g	

Vitamin A 4%	•	Vitamin C 21%	
Calcium 2%	•	Iron 11%	

Nutrition Grade A-
* Based on a 2000 calorie diet

Ingredients

- 2 pounds boneless pork loin or tenderloin, cut into 1-inch cubes
- 1/2 cup freshly squeezed orange juice
- 1/4 cup organic chicken broth

- 1 tart apple, peeled and diced
- 1/4 cup dried cherries
- 1/4 cup organic coconut flakes
- 1 small onion, chopped
- 1 clove garlic, minced
- 1/2 teaspoon ground ginger
- 1/4 teaspoon ground cinnamon
- 1/4 teaspoon sea salt

Directions
- Place pork cubes in a 5-quart slow cooker. In a medium bowl, mix all the other ingredients together. Pour the sauce over pork; mix well to coat.
- Cover and cook on Low for 5 to 6 hours, or until tender. Place pork on a plate and serve.

18. Slow Cooker Layered Meatloaf

Servings: 4-6
Preparation time: 15 minutes
Cook time: 2 hours 30 minutes on HIGH or 5 hours on LOW
Ready in: 2 hours and 45 minutes

Nutrition Facts
Serving Size 393 g

Amount Per Serving

Calories 375   Calories from Fat 133

	% Daily Value*
Total Fat 14.7g	**23%**
Saturated Fat 6.4g	**32%**
Trans Fat 0.3g	
Cholesterol 189mg	**63%**
Sodium 1135mg	**47%**
Total Carbohydrates 10.1g	**3%**
Dietary Fiber 2.7g	**11%**
Sugars 4.0g	
Protein 48.6g	

Vitamin A 5%	•	Vitamin C 29%	
Calcium 5%	•	Iron 40%	

Nutrition Grade B+
* Based on a 2000 calorie diet

Ingredients

Meatloaf:

- 2 pounds extra-lean grass fed ground beef
- 2 eggs
- 1 teaspoon ground black pepper
- 1 teaspoon sea salt
- 1/2 teaspoon smoked paprika
- 2 teaspoon granulated onion
- 1 cup fresh mushrooms, sliced
- 4 cloves garlic, crushed
- 1 teaspoon coconut oil, for greasing

Filling:

- Handful of fresh spinach leaves
- 1 cup sweet pickles
- 1 large white onion, sliced thin
- 1/2 cup pickled jalapenos
- 2 large fresh tomatoes, sliced
- 1/2 cup Dijon mustard

Topping:

- ¼ cup paleo ketchup (see Recipe No. 61)
- ¼ cup dried onion flakes

Directions

- Combine all meatloaf ingredients in a large bowl. Lightly grease the bottom of a 5-quart slow cooker with coconut oil.
- Divide meat mixture into thirds. Form each portion into a loaf and press one loaf into the slow cooker. Top the first layer with spinach leaves, sweet pickles, and onion slices. Spread 1/4 cup mustard evenly on top. Place another loaf on top. Top with pickled jalapenos and fresh tomato slices. Spread the remaining mustard evenly on top.
- Cover with the third loaf and spread evenly with ketchup. Sprinkle on dried onion flakes for garnish.
- Cook for 2 hours and 30 minutes on High, or 5 hours on Low. Serve with paleo ketchup.

19. Crock Pot Spicy Cilantro-Lime Chicken

Servings: 4-6

Preparation time: 2 hours and 15 minutes

Cook time: 6-8 hours on LOW

Ready in: 8 hours and 15 minutes

Nutrition Facts

Serving Size 194 g

Amount Per Serving

Calories 355	Calories from Fat 227

% Daily Value*

Total Fat 25.2g	**39%**
Saturated Fat 0.6g	**3%**
Cholesterol 0mg	**0%**
Sodium 490mg	**20%**
Total Carbohydrates 5.7g	**2%**
Dietary Fiber 1.4g	**5%**
Sugars 0.8g	
Protein 30.8g	

Vitamin A 23%	Vitamin C 21%
Calcium 2%	Iron 5%

Nutrition Grade C

* Based on a 2000 calorie diet

Ingredients

- 1 (6 pound) free-range organic whole chicken
- 1 teaspoon black pepper
- 1 teaspoon sea salt
- 1 teaspoon ground cumin
- 1 tablespoon chili powder
- 1 tablespoon cayenne
- 1/2 cup fresh lime juice
- 2 handfuls fresh cilantro
- 3 cloves garlic, crushed
- 1 tablespoon olive oil

Directions

- Wash and dry the chicken. Puncture the chicken with a knife or fork. Place in a large bowl and season with salt and pepper.
- In a small bowl, mix the chili powder, cayenne, and cumin; rub into the chicken to coat.

- To make the marinade, puree lime juice, cilantro, garlic, and olive oil in a food processor or blender.
- Put chicken and marinade in a zip-lock bag, squeeze contents a bit, release the air and seal it. Place it in the fridge and marinate for at least 2 hours or overnight, for best flavor.
- Pull chicken out of the bag and place in a 6 quart slow cooker. Pour marinade over chicken, including inside the cavity.
- Cook on Low for 6 to 8 hours. Best served with baked cauliflower and/or sautéed veggies.

20. Easy Paleo Crock Pot Chicken Curry with Peppers and Cabbage

Servings: 8
Preparation time: 10 minutes
Cook time: 4 hours on LOW
Ready in: 4 hours and 10 minutes

Nutrition Facts

Serving Size 328 g

Amount Per Serving

Calories 361 — Calories from Fat 248

	% Daily Value*
Total Fat 27.6g	42%
Saturated Fat 19.1g	96%
Cholesterol 0mg	0%
Sodium 151mg	6%
Total Carbohydrates 19.8g	7%
Dietary Fiber 6.4g	26%
Sugars 9.6g	
Protein 14.1g	

Vitamin A 40%	•	Vitamin C 191%
Calcium 6%	•	Iron 14%

Nutrition Grade B-

* Based on a 2000 calorie diet

Ingredients
- 2 pounds of boneless chicken thighs, cut into 1-inch cubes
- 2 tablespoons fresh ginger, chopped
- 2 cloves garlic, chopped
- 1 medium onion, diced

- 1/4 teaspoon sea salt
- 1/8 teaspoon ground black pepper
- 1 medium red bell pepper, diced
- 1 medium green bell pepper, diced
- 1/2 head of cabbage, cut into eighths
- 1 1/2 cups unsweetened light coconut milk (see Recipe No. 63)
- 1 tablespoon curry paste
- 1/4 cup cilantro leaves

Directions

- In a 4-quart slow cooker, combine chicken, ginger, garlic, onion, salt, and black pepper; toss to coat.
- In a small bowl, dissolve curry paste in coconut milk. Pour curry mixture over chicken mixture. Stir in bell peppers and cabbage.
- Cover and cook for 4 hours on Low.

21. Lemon Garlic Crock Pot Chicken

Servings: 6
Preparation time: 15 minutes
Cook time: 3 hours on HIGH or 6 hours on LOW
Ready in: 3 hours and 15 minutes

Nutrition Facts

Serving Size 129 g

Amount Per Serving

Calories 236	Calories from Fat 151

	% Daily Value*
Total Fat 16.8g	**26%**
Cholesterol 0mg	**0%**
Sodium 326mg	**14%**
Total Carbohydrates 3.8g	**1%**
Dietary Fiber 0.9g	**4%**
Sugars 0.6g	
Protein 20.5g	

Vitamin A 15%	•	Vitamin C 14%
Calcium 2%	•	Iron 4%

Nutrition Grade C

* Based on a 2000 calorie diet

Ingredients

- 1 teaspoon ground oregano
- 1/2 teaspoon sea salt
- 1/4 teaspoon ground black pepper
- 2 pounds skinless, boneless chicken breast halves
- 2 tablespoons olive oil
- 1/4 cup organic chicken broth
- 3 tablespoons fresh lemon juice
- 2 cloves garlic, minced
- 1 teaspoon fresh parsley, chopped
- 1 small sweet onion, chopped
- 1 teaspoon fresh basil, chopped

Directions

- Place chicken breasts in a large bowl. Mix oregano, salt, and pepper in a small bowl and rub into chicken.
- Heat olive oil in a skillet over medium heat.
- Add the chicken and cook for 3 to 5 minutes on each side, or until golden brown. Place chicken in a 5-quart slow cooker.
- Stir together the chicken broth, onion, lemon juice, basil, and garlic into the skillet; bring to a boil. Pour mixture over chicken in the slow cooker.
- Cover, and cook on High for 3 hours, or Low for 6 hours. Add the parsley before serving.

22. Slow Cooker Chicken Adobo with Swiss Chard

Servings: 4

Preparation time: 10 minutes Cook time: 8 hours on LOW and 5 minutes on HIGH

Ready in: 8 hours and 15 minutes

Nutrition Facts

Serving Size 287 g

Amount Per Serving

Calories 246   Calories from Fat 36

         % Daily Value*

Total Fat 4.0g	**6%**
Saturated Fat 0.8g	**4%**
Trans Fat 0.0g	
Cholesterol 99mg	**33%**
Sodium 306mg	**13%**
Total Carbohydrates 10.5g	**4%**
Dietary Fiber 2.1g	**8%**
Sugars 4.9g	
Protein 36.2g	

Vitamin A 24%	•	Vitamin C 19%
Calcium 3%	•	Iron 5%

Nutrition Grade B-

* Based on a 2000 calorie diet

Ingredients

- 2 onions, sliced
- 4 cloves garlic, crushed
- 1/2 cup apple cider vinegar
- 1/3 cup coconut aminos
- 1 tablespoon unrefined brown sugar
- 1 bay leaf
- 1 teaspoon peppercorns, crushed
- 1 1/2 pounds skinless, bone-in chicken thighs (about 8 thighs)
- 2 teaspoons paprika
- 1 medium head Swiss chard, cut into 1 1/2-inch strips
- 2 green onions, thinly sliced

Directions

- In a medium bowl, mix the onions, garlic, apple cider vinegar, coconut aminos, brown sugar, bay leaf, and peppercorns in a 5-quart slow cooker.
- Add chicken and toss to coat. Sprinkle paprika over chicken.
- Cover and cook on Low for 8 hours. Before serving, add the Swiss chard to chicken mixture. Cook for another 5 minutes on High, and then sprinkle with green onion.

23. Crock Pot Gingered Beef and Veggies

Servings: 6
Serving size: 1 medium bowl
Preparation Time: 25 minutes
Cook Time: 10-12 hours on LOW and 15 minutes on HIGH
Ready in: 10 hours and 40 minutes

Nutrition Facts

Serving Size 407 g

Amount Per Serving

Calories 369	Calories from Fat 124

	% Daily Value*
Total Fat 13.8g	**21%**
Saturated Fat 4.0g	**20%**
Trans Fat 0.0g	
Cholesterol 95mg	**32%**
Sodium 298mg	**12%**
Total Carbohydrates 20.5g	**7%**
Dietary Fiber 2.9g	**11%**
Sugars 5.5g	
Protein 38.6g	

Vitamin A 204%	•	Vitamin C 13%
Calcium 5%	•	Iron 22%

Nutrition Grade A-

* Based on a 2000 calorie diet

Ingredients
- 1-1/2 cups pure beef broth
- 3 tablespoon Coconut Aminos
- 1 tablespoon almond butter
- 1 teaspoon raw honey
- 1 teaspoon olive oil
- A pinch of white pepper
- 2 tablespoon grated ginger
- ¼ teaspoon pepper
- 1-1/2 lbs. boneless beef round steak, trimmed and cut into 1-inch cubes
- 4 carrots, sliced into ½-inch thick pieces
- 1 onion, chopped
- 4 cloves garlic, minced
- 3 tablespoon water
- 3 tablespoon arrowroot powder

Directions

- Stir together the first 8 ingredients in a small bowl until smooth. Place beef, carrots, onions and garlic in a 4-5 quart slow cooker.
- Pour the prepared ginger mixture over beef and vegetables. Place lid on slow cooker and cook on low for 10 to 12 hours or until beef and veggies are tender.
- Just before serving, combine arrowroot powder and water in a small bowl and stir into the slow cooker.
- Cover and cook on high for 15-20 minutes until thickened.

24. Slow Cooker Jalapeno Roast

Servings: 6-8
Preparation time: 10 minutes
Cook time: 8-9 hours on LOW
Ready in: 8 hours 10 minutes

Nutrition Facts

Serving Size 234 g

Amount Per Serving

Calories 239   Calories from Fat 92

         % Daily Value*

Total Fat 10.2g	**16%**
Saturated Fat 4.5g	**22%**
Trans Fat 0.0g	
Cholesterol 78mg	**26%**
Sodium 1063mg	**44%**
Total Carbohydrates 14.7g	**5%**
Dietary Fiber 3.3g	**13%**
Sugars 3.6g	
Protein 22.7g	

Vitamin A 6%	Vitamin C 8%
Calcium 1%	Iron 2%

Nutrition Grade D+

* Based on a 2000 calorie diet

Ingredients

- 1 (2.5 pounds) pot roast
- 5 fresh jalapeno peppers, seeded and quartered
- 1/2 teaspoon ground black pepper
- 1 teaspoon sea salt

- 1 large onion, cut into eights
- 2 cloves garlic, thinly sliced

Directions
- Place meat in a 5-6 quart slow cooker. Season lightly with salt and pepper on all sides.
- Cover with the jalapenos, onion and garlic.
- Cook on Low for 8-9 hours, or until tender.

25. Slow Cooker Herbs and Chicken Drumsticks

Servings: 5
Serving size: 2 chicken drumsticks
Preparation time: 10 minutes
Cook time: 4 hours on HIGH and 10 minutes
Ready in: 4 hours and 20 minutes

Nutrition Facts

Serving Size 183 g

Amount Per Serving

Calories 334	Calories from Fat 49

	% Daily Value*
Total Fat 5.4g	**8%**
Saturated Fat 1.4g	**7%**
Trans Fat 0.0g	
Cholesterol 81mg	**27%**
Sodium 197mg	**8%**
Total Carbohydrates 46.5g	**15%**
Sugars 42.1g	
Protein 25.9g	

Vitamin A 1%	•	Vitamin C 7%
Calcium 3%	•	Iron 10%

Nutrition Grade B+
* Based on a 2000 calorie diet

Ingredients
- 6 garlic cloves, minced
- 2 tablespoons fresh grated ginger
- 10 lemongrass leaves, finely sliced
- 1/2 cup unrefined brown sugar
- 1/8 teaspoon black pepper
- 2 teaspoons chili sauce

- 1/2 cup raw honey
- 1/3 cup balsamic vinegar
- 1/3 cup Coconut Aminos
- 2 teaspoons chili sauce
- 10 chicken drumsticks, skin removed and discarded

Directions
- Place a saucepan over medium heat. Stir in all the ingredients except the chicken. Bring to a boil, and then simmer for 5 minutes over low heat, until the sauce is beginning to thicken. Remove from heat and cool for a few minutes.
- Place chicken drumsticks in a 6-quart slow cooker and pour the sauce over; toss to coat.
- Cover and cook on High for 4 hours. Serve with your choice of sautéed veggies.

26. Crock Pot Balsamic Seared Pork Roast

Servings: 5-6
Preparation time: 10 minutes
Cook time: 6 hours on LOW and 8 minutes
Ready in: 6 hours and 18 minutes

Nutrition Facts

Serving Size 368 g

Amount Per Serving

Calories 487   Calories from Fat 194

% Daily Value*

Total Fat 21.6g	**33%**
Saturated Fat 10.3g	**52%**
Trans Fat 0.0g	
Cholesterol 152mg	**51%**
Sodium 380mg	**16%**
Total Carbohydrates 10.0g	**3%**
Dietary Fiber 1.4g	**6%**
Sugars 6.2g	
Protein 58.6g	

Vitamin A 4%	•	Vitamin C 11%
Calcium 2%	•	Iron 30%

Nutrition Grade B

* Based on a 2000 calorie diet

Ingredients

- 1 (2-pound) top round roast
- 3/4 cup balsamic vinegar
- 2 large sweet onions, sliced
- 1 cup pure beef broth
- 2 tablespoon coconut oil
- 1/2 teaspoon garlic powder
- 1/2 teaspoon onion powder
- 1/2 teaspoon smoked paprika
- 1 tablespoon raw honey
- 1/2 teaspoon sea salt
- 1/2 teaspoon red pepper flakes

Directions

- In a small bowl, mix together the garlic and onion powder, paprika, honey, salt, and pepper. Pour mixture over roast and thoroughly rub on both sides.
- Place a large skillet over medium-high heat. Add the coconut oil when skillet is hot. Add the roast and sear each side for 3 minutes.
- Spread the sliced onions in the bottom of a 6-quart crock pot. Place the seared meat on top of the onions.
- In a bowl, combine the balsamic vinegar and beef broth, and then pour over the meat.
- Cover the slow cooker and cook on Low for 6-8 hours.

27. Slow Cooked Rump Roast

Servings: 8
Preparation time: 10 minutes
Cook time: 10 hours on LOW
Ready in: 10 hours 10 minutes

Nutrition Facts

Serving Size 150 g

Amount Per Serving

Calories 178   Calories from Fat 58

	% Daily Value*
Total Fat 6.4g	**10%**
Saturated Fat 2.1g	**10%**
Cholesterol 75mg	**25%**
Sodium 121mg	**5%**
Total Carbohydrates 3.4g	**1%**
Dietary Fiber 1.3g	**5%**
Sugars 0.9g	
Protein 25.8g	

Vitamin A 14%	•	Vitamin C 5%
Calcium 3%	•	Iron 19%

Nutrition Grade C+

* Based on a 2000 calorie diet

Ingredients

- 1 tablespoon paprika
- 1/2 teaspoon cayenne
- 1/2 teaspoon garlic, chopped
- 1/4 teaspoon mustard powder
- 1 teaspoon caraway seed
- 1/4 teaspoon dried rosemary
- 1 tablespoon ground black pepper
- 2 teaspoon chili powder
- 1 (2-3 pounds) grass-fed rump roast
- 1 large onion, diced
- 1/2 cup organic beef stock

Directions

- Mix together the first 8 ingredients in a bowl. Rub the spice mixture all over the rump roast to coat. Spread the onions evenly in the bottom of a 5-quart slow cooker.
- Place the seasoned roast on top of the onions and cover with beef stock.
- Cover and cook for 10 hours on Low.

28. Crock Pot Hot Chicken Barbecue

Servings: 8

Preparation time: 10 minutes

Cook time: 6 hours on LOW

Ready in: 6 hours and 10 minutes

Nutrition Facts

Serving Size 172 g

Amount Per Serving	
Calories 328	Calories from Fat 114
	% Daily Value*
Total Fat 12.7g	**20%**
Saturated Fat 3.5g	**17%**
Cholesterol 151mg	**50%**
Sodium 383mg	**16%**
Total Carbohydrates 1.1g	**0%**
Protein 49.4g	

Vitamin A 8%	•	Vitamin C 1%
Calcium 3%	•	Iron 14%

Nutrition Grade B

* Based on a 2000 calorie diet

Ingredients

- 2 teaspoon paprika
- 1 teaspoon onion powder
- 1 teaspoon dried thyme
- 1 teaspoon ground white pepper
- 1/2 teaspoon chili powder
- 1/2 teaspoon garlic powder
- 1/2 teaspoon ground black pepper
- 1 teaspoon sea salt
- 1 (3-pound) whole chicken, cleaned
- 1 lemon, sliced

Directions

- Pat dry chicken with paper towels. Combine the first 8 ingredients in a small bowl. Thoroughly rub mixture all over the chicken.
- Place the seasoned chicken in a 6-quart slow cooker. Place the lemon slices on top of the chicken.

- Cover the slow cooker, set to low, and cook chicken for 6 hours. Serve with sautéed veggies on the side.

29. Hot Wings from the Crock Pot

Servings: 10

Serving size: 1 hot chicken wing

Preparation time: 10 minutes

Cook time: 6 hours on LOW and 5 minutes on HIGH

Ready in: 6 hours and 15 minutes

Nutrition Facts

Serving Size 105 g

Amount Per Serving

Calories 190	Calories from Fat 75

% Daily Value*

Total Fat 8.4g	**13%**
Saturated Fat 3.6g	**18%**
Trans Fat 0.0g	
Cholesterol 73mg	**24%**
Sodium 227mg	**9%**
Total Carbohydrates 2.7g	**1%**
Dietary Fiber 1.2g	**5%**
Protein 24.3g	

Vitamin A 2%	•	Vitamin C 1%
Calcium 2%	•	Iron 9%

Nutrition Grade B-

* Based on a 2000 calorie diet

Ingredients
- 10 chicken wings
- 1/2 cup Coconut butter
- 1/2 cup Paleo hot sauce (Frank's, Trader Joe's, etc.)
- 1/4 cup organic chicken broth
- 3 tablespoons black pepper
- 1/2 teaspoon cayenne pepper
- 1/2 teaspoon mustard
- 1/2 teaspoon of garlic powder

Directions
- In a mixing bowl, combine coconut butter, hot sauce, and broth. Mix the remaining ingredients in a small bowl.

- Place chicken wings in a 6-quart crock pot and season each side with the mixed spices. Pour the hot sauce mixture over chicken. Cook covered on Low for 6 hours.
- Remove chicken from the crock pot and place on a baking sheet. Pour the sauce in a saucepan and simmer over medium heat until beginning to thicken. Pour sauce over chicken.
- Broil chicken wings in the oven on High for 3-5 minutes.

30. Herbed Pork Loin and Squash Stew

Servings: 8

Serving size: 1 medium bowl

Preparation time: 10 minutes

Cook time: 5 hours on HIGH or 7 hours on LOW

Ready in: 5 hours and 10 minutes

Nutrition Facts

Serving Size 294 g

Amount Per Serving

Calories 526   Calories from Fat 336

	% Daily Value*
Total Fat 37.3g	**57%**
Saturated Fat 14.9g	**74%**
Cholesterol 122mg	**41%**
Sodium 216mg	**9%**
Total Carbohydrates 12.9g	**4%**
Dietary Fiber 2.5g	**10%**
Sugars 3.2g	
Protein 34.0g	

Vitamin A 156%   •   Vitamin C 36%

Calcium 9%   •   Iron 13%

Nutrition Grade B

* Based on a 2000 calorie diet

Ingredients
- 1/4 teaspoon black pepper
- 1/4 teaspoon dried rosemary
- 1/4 teaspoon ground cumin
- 1/4 teaspoon paprika
- 1 bay leaf
- 1 teaspoons sea salt, or to taste
- 2 1/2 pounds pork loin chops, cubed

- 1 cup Swiss chard leaves, chopped
- 4 celery stalks, chopped
- 2 medium onions, diced
- 8 garlic cloves, thinly sliced
- 4 cups butternut squash, peeled and cubed
- 1 teaspoon fresh squeezed lemon juice
- 1/4 cup full-fat coconut milk (see Recipe No. 63)
- 1 cup organic chicken broth

Directions

- In a small bowl, combine the first 6 ingredients.
- Place the vegetables and pork into a 6-quart slow cooker and sprinkle with the spice mixture; toss to coat. Pour in the lemon juice, coconut milk, and chicken broth; mix well.
- Cover and cook for 5 hours on High, or 7 hours on Low.

31. Crock Pot Pork Chops

Servings: 4
Serving size: 1 thick cut pork chop
Preparation time: 10 minutes
Cook time: 4 hours on HIGH
Ready in: 4 hours and 10 minutes

Nutrition Facts

Serving Size 317 g

Amount Per Serving

Calories 512　　　　　Calories from Fat 321

	% Daily Value*
Total Fat 35.7g	55%
Saturated Fat 13.4g	67%
Trans Fat 0.0g	
Cholesterol 122mg	41%
Sodium 234mg	10%
Total Carbohydrates 13.1g	4%
Dietary Fiber 2.4g	10%
Sugars 3.2g	
Protein 33.8g	

Vitamin A 157%　　•　　Vitamin C 41%
Calcium 9%　　•　　Iron 12%

Nutrition Grade B
* Based on a 2000 calorie diet

Ingredients

- 1 cup pure low-sodium vegetable broth
- 1/4 cup olive oil
- 3 cloves garlic, minced
- 1 tablespoon paprika
- 1 tablespoon onion, minced
- 1/2 teaspoon ground mustard
- 1 teaspoon dried basil
- 1 teaspoon dried thyme
- 4 thick cut boneless pork chops
- sea salt and pepper to taste

Directions

- In a large bowl, combine the vegetable broth, olive oil, garlic, paprika, onion, mustard, basil, and thyme. Using a sharp, pointed knife cut small slits in each pork chop and season with sea salt and pepper.
- Place pork chops into a 4-quart slow cooker. Pour the prepared sauce over the pork chops.
- Cover and cook on High for 4 hours.

32. Slowly-But-Surely Crock Pot Pernil Pork

Servings: 8-10
Preparation time: 10 minutes
Cook time: 6-8 hours on LOW
Ready in: 6 hours and 10 minutes

Nutrition Facts

Serving Size 197 g

Amount Per Serving

Calories 266   Calories from Fat 62

	% Daily Value*
Total Fat 6.9g	**11%**
Saturated Fat 2.2g	**11%**
Trans Fat 0.1g	
Cholesterol 124mg	**41%**
Sodium 567mg	**24%**
Total Carbohydrates 3.6g	**1%**
Dietary Fiber 1.0g	**4%**
Sugars 0.8g	
Protein 45.1g	

Vitamin A 3%	•	Vitamin C 5%
Calcium 3%	•	Iron 16%

Nutrition Grade A-

* Based on a 2000 calorie diet

Ingredients

- 5 cloves garlic, minced
- 1 large onion, halved
- 1 tablespoon ground oregano
- 1 tablespoon ground cumin
- 1 teaspoon cayenne pepper
- 1/2 teaspoon cinnamon
- 2 teaspoons sea salt
- 2 teaspoons ground black pepper
- 1 teaspoon olive oil
- 1 tablespoon white wine vinegar
- 1 (3 pound) boneless pork loin roast
- 1 lemon, sliced into wedges

Directions

- Place pork in the bottom of a 6-quart slow cooker. Combine the first 10 ingredients in a bowl and rub into pork.
- Cook on Low for 6 to 8 hours, or until tender. Once cooked, shred the pork and garnish with lemon wedges to serve.

DINNER

33. Crock Pot Picante Short Ribs

Servings: 6

Preparation time: 10 minutes

Cook time: 8-9 hours on LOW and 35 minutes

Ready in: 8 hours and 45 minutes

Nutrition Facts

Serving Size 386 g

Amount Per Serving

Calories 586	Calories from Fat 228

	% Daily Value*
Total Fat 25.3g	**39%**
Saturated Fat 9.7g	**48%**
Trans Fat 0.0g	
Cholesterol 130mg	**43%**
Sodium 1407mg	**59%**
Total Carbohydrates 52.8g	**18%**
Dietary Fiber 1.5g	**6%**
Sugars 30.8g	
Protein 44.3g	

Vitamin A 16%	•	Vitamin C 25%
Calcium 7%	•	Iron 30%

Nutrition Grade D+

* Based on a 2000 calorie diet

Ingredients

- 1 tablespoon olive oil
- 3.5-4 pounds bone-in beef short ribs cut into serving-sized pieces
- 1 large onion, sliced
- 4 cloves garlic, crushed
- 2 cups organic picante sauce
- 2 tablespoons unrefined brown sugar
- 2 tablespoons arrowroot powder
- 2 tablespoons lemon zest
- 2 tablespoons fresh rosemary, chopped

Directions

- Place a large skillet over medium-high heat. Once hot, add the olive oil. Add the beef and cook until evenly brown. Remove from heat and set aside.

- In a medium bowl, combine the picante sauce and brown sugar. Line the bottom of a 5-quart slow cooker with the onion and garlic. Top with the beef. Pour the prepared picante sauce mixture over the beef.

- Cook covered on Low for 8-9 hours or until the beef is fork-tender. Transfer beef onto a plate and keep warm.

- Stir the arrowroot powder in the cooked picante sauce. Cover and cook on High for 10 minutes, or until the mixture is thick. Pour sauce over beef and garnish with lemon zest and fresh chopped rosemary.

34. Slow Cooker Beef Stew

Servings: 6
Serving size: 1 medium bowl
Preparation time: 15 minutes
Cook time: 4-6 hours on HIGH, or 10-12 hours on LOW
Ready in: 4 hours and 15 minutes

Nutrition Facts

Serving Size 333 g

Amount Per Serving

Calories 336 | Calories from Fat 92

	% Daily Value*
Total Fat 10.2g	**16%**
Saturated Fat 4.1g	**21%**
Trans Fat 0.0g	
Cholesterol 135mg	**45%**
Sodium 399mg	**17%**
Total Carbohydrates 9.5g	**3%**
Dietary Fiber 3.3g	**13%**
Sugars 3.2g	
Protein 48.3g	

Vitamin A 144%	•	Vitamin C 15%
Calcium 3%	•	Iron 164%

Nutrition Grade A-

* Based on a 2000 calorie diet

Ingredients

- 2 pounds beef stew meat, cut into 1 inch cubes
- 3 tablespoons coconut flour
- 1/2 teaspoon sea salt
- 1/2 teaspoon ground black pepper
- 1 teaspoon Paleo Worcestershire sauce (see Recipe No. 62)
- 1 onion, chopped
- 2 clove garlic, minced
- 1 teaspoon paprika
- 2 bay leaves
- 1 cup button mushrooms, quartered
- 4 carrots, sliced
- 1 stalk celery, chopped
- 1 1/2 cups pure beef broth
- 1/4 cup fresh parsley, chopped

Directions

- Place beef in a 4-quart slow cooker. Combine the coconut flour, sea salt, and pepper in a small bowl. Pour the flour mixture over beef; toss to coat. Add the remaining ingredients and stir well.
- Cook covered for 4 to 6 hours on High, or 10 to 12 hours on Low. Serve warm topped with chopped fresh parsley.

35. Crock Pot Beef and Veggie Chili

Servings: 8
Serving size: 1 medium bowl
Preparation time: 10 minutes
Cook time: 8 hours on LOW and 15 minutes
Ready in: 8 hours and 25 minutes

Nutrition Facts

Serving Size 456 g

Amount Per Serving

Calories 241   Calories from Fat 68

	% Daily Value*
Total Fat 7.6g	**12%**
Saturated Fat 3.2g	**16%**
Trans Fat 0.0g	
Cholesterol 50mg	**17%**
Sodium 589mg	**25%**
Total Carbohydrates 23.7g	**8%**
Dietary Fiber 6.3g	**25%**
Sugars 12.2g	
Protein 20.2g	

Vitamin A 59%	•	Vitamin C 134%
Calcium 5%	•	Iron 16%

Nutrition Grade A-

* Based on a 2000 calorie diet

Ingredients

- 1 pound lean grass-fed ground beef
- 2 medium onions, chopped
- 3 cloves garlic, minced
- 1 large green bell pepper, chopped
- 1 large yellow bell pepper, chopped
- 1 cup zucchini, chopped
- 3/4 cup diced celery
- 3 1/2 cup (about 28 ounce) tomato puree (recommended: Mr. Organic)
- 1 3/4 cup (about 14 ounce) tomato sauce (recommended: Tropical Traditions)
- 1 1/2 cups pure beef broth
- 3 tablespoon chili powder
- 1 teaspoon dried basil
- 1 teaspoon oregano
- 1 teaspoon garlic powder
- 1 teaspoon onion powder
- 1 teaspoon sea salt
- 1 teaspoon pepper

Directions

- Place a skillet over medium heat. Add the ground beef and cook until brown. Discard grease.
- Place cooked beef in a 4-quart slow cooker. Stir in the remaining ingredients. Mix well.
- Cook covered on Low for 8 hours.

36. Slow Cooked Roast Beef N' Veggies

Servings: 6-8

Preparation time: 10 minutes

Cook time: 5-6 hours on HIGH

Ready in: 5 hours and 10 minutes

Nutrition Facts

Serving Size 457 g

Amount Per Serving

Calories 862   Calories from Fat 570

% Daily Value*

Total Fat 63.3g   **97%**

Saturated Fat 25.2g   **126%**

Trans Fat 0.0g

Cholesterol 234mg   **78%**

Sodium 344mg   **14%**

Total Carbohydrates 7.5g   **2%**

Dietary Fiber 1.7g   **7%**

Sugars 2.8g

Protein 61.4g

Vitamin A 103%   •   Vitamin C 6%

Calcium 6%   •   Iron 43%

Nutrition Grade C+

* Based on a 2000 calorie diet

Ingredients

- 3 pounds beef chuck roast
- 1/3 cup Coconut Aminos
- 1 teaspoon turmeric
- 1 teaspoon celery salt
- 7 teaspoons dried onion flakes
- 1 teaspoon onion powder
- 2 1/4 teaspoons freshly ground black pepper
- 3 carrots, sliced into chunks
- 2 cups fresh cremini mushrooms, halved

- 1 sprig fresh rosemary
- 2 bay leaves
- 2 1/2 cups pure beef broth

Directions

- Combine the coconut aminos, turmeric, celery salt, onion flakes, onion powder, and 1/4 teaspoon pepper in a small bowl.
- Place the carrots and mushrooms in the bottom of a 5-quart slow cooker. Place the roast over the vegetables, and then add rosemary and bay leaves.
- Pour the prepared coconut aminos mixture over the roast, and then add the beef broth. Sprinkle 2 teaspoons of fresh ground pepper over the top.
- Cover the slow cooker, and cook the roast for 5-6 hours on High. Set slow cooker to Low for the last 2 hours.

37. Slow Cooker Lettuce-Wrapped Pork Carnitas

Servings: 8-10
Preparation time: 10 minutes
Cook time: 10 hours on LOW
Ready in: 10 hours and 10 minutes

Nutrition Facts

Serving Size 314 g

Amount Per Serving

Calories 517　　　　Calories from Fat 363

% Daily Value*

Total Fat 40.3g	**62%**
Saturated Fat 13.4g	**67%**
Cholesterol 128mg	**43%**
Sodium 619mg	**26%**
Total Carbohydrates 4.4g	**1%**
Dietary Fiber 2.2g	**9%**
Sugars 1.6g	
Protein 32.5g	

Vitamin A 4%	•	Vitamin C 25%
Calcium 2%	•	Iron 14%

Nutrition Grade D+

* Based on a 2000 calorie diet

Ingredients

- 4 cloves garlic, minced
- 1 teaspoon sea salt
- 1 teaspoon dried sage
- 1/2 teaspoon ground coriander
- 1/2 teaspoon crumbled dried oregano
- 1 (4-pound) boneless pork shoulder roast, cut into large chunks
- 2 cups organic chicken broth
- 1/4 cup organic chili sauce
- 1 head of butter lettuce
- 2 bay leaves
- 2 medium tomatoes, diced, (optional)
- 1 large avocado, sliced into 1/2-inch chunks (optional)

Directions
- In a small bowl, combine the garlic, sea salt, sage, coriander, and dried oregano. Sprinkle spice mixture over the pork chunks and toss to coat.
- Place pork in the bottom of a 5-quart slow cooker. Pour the chicken broth and add the bay leaves. Cook covered on Low for 10 hours, or until fork tender. Flip pork over half way through cooking.
- Transfer pork to a plate and shred pork using 2 forks. Spoon shredded pork mixture in lettuce leaves, and then add the diced tomatoes and avocado chunks.

38. Slow Cooker Sweet Barbecue Ribs

Servings: 8
Preparation time: 10 minutes
Cook time: 6-8 hours on LOW and 30 minutes
Ready in: 6 hours and 40 minutes

Nutrition Facts

Serving Size 272 g

Amount Per Serving

Calories 784   Calories from Fat 488

	% Daily Value*
Total Fat 54.2g	**83%**
Saturated Fat 21.8g	**109%**
Trans Fat 0.0g	
Cholesterol 154mg	**51%**
Sodium 1007mg	**42%**
Total Carbohydrates 29.2g	**10%**
Dietary Fiber 0.8g	**3%**
Sugars 20.8g	
Protein 41.5g	

Vitamin A 12%	•	Vitamin C 5%
Calcium 4%	•	Iron 26%

Nutrition Grade C

* Based on a 2000 calorie diet

Ingredients

- 4 pounds pork baby back ribs
- 2 cups Paleo Barbecue sauce (see Recipe No. 64)
- 1 cup Paleo Ketchup (see Recipe No. 61)
- 1/2 cup unrefined brown sugar
- 3 tablespoons apple cider vinegar
- 2 teaspoons dried oregano
- 1 tablespoon garlic salt
- 2 tablespoons onion powder
- 1 tablespoon black pepper
- 1 pinch sea salt

Directions

- Preheat oven to 400 degrees F. Combine garlic salt, onion powder and pepper in a small bowl. Season ribs with the spice mixture.
- Place ribs in a baking pan and brown in oven 15 minutes on each side; drain fat.
- In a medium bowl, mix together the barbecue sauce, ketchup, brown sugar, vinegar, oregano, and salt to taste.
- Place ribs in a 5-quart slow cooker. Pour prepared sauce over ribs, and turn to coat.
- Cook ribs covered on Low for 6 to 8 hours, or until tender.

39. Slow Cooker Turkey Breast

Servings: 12

Preparation time: 10 minutes

Cook time: 1 hour on HIGH and 7 hours on LOW

Ready in: 8 hours and 10 minutes

Nutrition Facts

Serving Size 214 g

Amount Per Serving

Calories 268	Calories from Fat 13

% Daily Value*

Total Fat 1.5g	**2%**
Trans Fat 0.0g	
Cholesterol 157mg	**52%**
Sodium 128mg	**5%**
Total Carbohydrates 2.9g	**1%**
Dietary Fiber 0.6g	**2%**
Sugars 1.2g	
Protein 57.2g	

Vitamin A 35%	•	Vitamin C 3%
Calcium 3%	•	Iron 17%

Nutrition Grade A

* Based on a 2000 calorie diet

Ingredients

- 1 (5-6 pound) bone-in lean turkey breast, rinsed and pat dried
- 1 teaspoon turmeric
- 1 teaspoon celery salt
- 7 teaspoons dried onion flakes
- 1 teaspoon onion powder
- 1/4 teaspoons freshly ground black pepper
- 3 celery stalks, diced
- 2 medium carrots, diced
- 1 sweet yellow onion, diced
- 1/2 tablespoon minced garlic, minced
- 1/4 cup pure chicken broth

Directions

- Mix together all the turmeric, celery salt, onion flakes, onion powder, and black pepper in a small bowl. Rub spice mixture all over the turkey.

- In a 6-quart slow cooker, layer the celery, carrots, onion, and garlic; cover with chicken broth. Place turkey on top of the vegetables.
- Place lid on slow cooker, and cook turkey and vegetables for 1 hour on High, then set to Low, and cook for 7 hours.

40. Slow-Cooked Herbed Citrus Salmon

Servings: 6
Serving size: 1 fillet
Preparation time: 10 minutes
Cook time: 1 hour and 15 minutes on LOW
Ready in: 1 hour and 10 minutes

Nutrition Facts

Serving Size 200 g

Amount Per Serving

Calories 427	Calories from Fat 274
	% Daily Value*
Total Fat 30.4g	47%
Saturated Fat 5.5g	27%
Cholesterol 95mg	32%
Sodium 329mg	14%
Total Carbohydrates 3.4g	1%
Dietary Fiber 0.7g	3%
Sugars 1.3g	
Protein 33.9g	

Vitamin A 6%	•	Vitamin C 22%
Calcium 3%	•	Iron 4%

Nutrition Grade B
* Based on a 2000 calorie diet

Ingredients
- 1 tablespoon olive oil (for greasing)
- 1 large onion, thinly sliced
- 2 pounds salmon fillets cut in 6 fillets
- 2 tablespoons extra virgin olive oil
- 3 garlic cloves, crushed and finely chopped
- 1 cup cilantro leaves, chopped
- 3/4 teaspoon sea salt
- 1/2 teaspoon freshly ground black pepper
- 2 tablespoons extra virgin olive oil

- 1 tablespoon fresh lemon juice
- 1 tablespoon fresh orange juice
- 1/2 teaspoon grated lemon zest
- 1/2 teaspoon grated orange zest
- Salt and freshly ground black pepper
- 1 tablespoon chopped fresh flat leaf parsley

Directions

- Coat the bottom of a 5-quart slow cooker with olive oil. Spread onion slices in the bottom slow cooker.
- In a small bowl, stir together the 2 tablespoons olive oil, garlic, cilantro, sea salt, and pepper, and then rub into the salmon fillets. Place the salmon in the slow cooker, skin side down.
- Cover and cook for 1 hour and 15 minutes on Low, or until cooked through. Place salmon fillets onto serving plates. Mix together the remaining ingredients in a small bowl and spread on top of each fillet.

41. Slow Cooked Spicy Salsa Chicken Shreds

Servings: 3
Preparation time: 10 minutes
Cook time: 4-5 hours on LOW
Ready in: 4 hours and 10 minutes

Nutrition Facts

Serving Size 278 g

Amount Per Serving

Calories 203	Calories from Fat 31

	% Daily Value*
Total Fat 3.4g	5%
Saturated Fat 0.6g	3%
Cholesterol 65mg	22%
Sodium 464mg	19%
Total Carbohydrates 16.1g	5%
Dietary Fiber 4.6g	18%
Sugars 8.7g	
Protein 25.7g	

Vitamin A 40%	•	Vitamin C 48%
Calcium 2%	•	Iron 15%

Nutrition Grade B+

* Based on a 2000 calorie diet

Ingredients

- 2 medium fresh tomatoes, peeled and coarsely chopped
- 1 small sweet onion, chopped
- 1/2 cup green chilies, diced
- 1-1/2 teaspoons unrefined brown sugar
- 1/4 teaspoon garlic powder
- 1/8 teaspoon ground cumin
- 1/8 teaspoon dried cilantro
- 3 skinless, boneless chicken breast halves
- 1/4 cup organic tomato sauce (recommended: Tropical Traditions)
- 1 small red onion, chopped
- 1 teaspoon chili powder
- 3 cloves garlic, minced
- 1 teaspoon ground cumin
- 1 medium Jalapeno, chopped
- 1/4 teaspoon sea salt
- 1/8 teaspoon fresh ground pepper, or to taste

Directions

- To make the salsa, mix together the first 7 ingredients in a small bowl.

- Place the chicken breasts in the bottom of a 4-quart slow cooker, and pour in the prepared salsa and tomato sauce. Add the onion, chili powder, garlic, cumin, Jalapeno, sea salt, and pepper.
- Cover, and cook for 4-5 hours on Low, or until fork tender. Shred the chicken using two forks. Transfer shredded chicken to plates and serve.

42. Slow Cooker Pork Chile Verde

Servings: 8-10
Serving size: 1 medium bowl
Preparation time: 10 minutes
Cook time: 3 hours on HIGH and 4-5 hours on LOW and 15 minutes
Ready in: 7 hours and 25 minutes

Nutrition Facts

Serving Size 355 g

Amount Per Serving

Calories 348   Calories from Fat 114

	% Daily Value*
Total Fat 12.7g	**19%**
Saturated Fat 2.8g	**14%**
Trans Fat 0.1g	
Cholesterol 124mg	**41%**
Sodium 209mg	**9%**
Total Carbohydrates 11.7g	**4%**
Dietary Fiber 3.7g	**15%**
Sugars 2.0g	
Protein 46.4g	

Vitamin A 8%	•	Vitamin C 41%
Calcium 4%	•	Iron 22%

Nutrition Grade A
* Based on a 2000 calorie diet

Ingredients
Green Salsa:
- 2 pounds tomatillos, husked
- 1 cup onion, chopped
- 2 teaspoon garlic, minced
- 2 chili peppers, minced
- 3 tablespoons fresh cilantro leaves, chopped
- 2 tablespoon fresh oregano, chopped

- 1/2 teaspoon ground cumin
- 1 1/2 teaspoons sea salt, or to taste
- 1 tablespoon fresh lime juice

Pork sauté:
- 3 pounds boneless pork shoulder, cubed
- 3 tablespoons olive oil
- 1/2 cup onion, chopped
- 2 cloves garlic, minced
- 1/2 cup jalapeno peppers, diced
- 1 3/4 cup tomatoes, diced

Directions
- Place all the green salsa ingredients in a blender and blend it all together. Transfer puree into a saucepan and cook over medium heat for 15 minutes, or until smooth. Remove from heat and set aside.
- Place a large skillet over medium heat. Once hot, add the olive oil. Sauté onion and garlic until fragrant. Add the pork, and cook until browned.
- Place the cooked pork, onions and garlic, jalapeno peppers, and tomatoes into a 5-quart slow cooker. Pour in the prepared green salsa.
- Cook covered for 3 hours on High. Switch to Low, and then cook for 4 to 5 hours.

43. Crock Pot Lemon N' Lime Fish Fillets

Servings: 5
Serving size: 1 fillet
Preparation time: 10 minutes
Cook time: 1 hour 30 minutes on LOW
Ready in: 1 hour 40 minutes

Nutrition Facts

Serving Size 198 g

Amount Per Serving

Calories 230	Calories from Fat 122

	% Daily Value*
Total Fat 13.5g	**21%**
Saturated Fat 2.4g	**12%**
Cholesterol 64mg	**21%**
Sodium 174mg	**7%**
Total Carbohydrates 5.4g	**2%**
Dietary Fiber 1.5g	**6%**
Sugars 1.2g	
Protein 22.0g	

Vitamin A 12%	•	Vitamin C 41%
Calcium 5%	•	Iron 13%

Nutrition Grade A-

* Based on a 2000 calorie diet

Ingredients

- 1 1/2 pounds catfish fillets (or other white fish)
- 1/4 teaspoon sea salt
- 1/4 teaspoon pepper
- 1/4 cup fresh lemon juice
- 1/2 cup onion, chopped
- 5 tablespoons fresh parsley, chopped
- 2 tablespoons fresh dill, chopped
- 1 tablespoon olive oil
- olive oil spray
- 2 teaspoons grated lemon rind
- 2 teaspoons grated lime rind
- lemon and lime slices
- 8 fresh parsley sprigs

Directions

- Spray the inside of a 4-quart slow cooker with olive oil spray. Place fish fillets in the slow cooker; season with salt and pepper. Drizzle fillets with lemon juice.
- Sprinkle the onion, parsley, grated lemon and lime rind, and olive oil over fish.

- Place lid on slow cooker and cook fish fillets on Low for 1 hour and 30 minutes. Garnish with and lemon and lime slices and sprigs of fresh parsley to serve.

44. Asian Crock Pot Beef Spare Ribs

Servings: 8-12
Preparation time: 8 hours 10 minutes
Cook time: 6-8 hours on LOW
Ready in: 14 hours and 10 minutes

Nutrition Facts

Serving Size 203 g

Amount Per Serving

Calories 613   Calories from Fat 505

% **Daily Value***

Total Fat 56.1g	**86%**
Saturated Fat 24.3g	**121%**
Trans Fat 0.0g	
Cholesterol 114mg	**38%**
Sodium 148mg	**6%**
Total Carbohydrates 3.4g	**1%**
Sugars 1.8g	
Protein 21.6g	

Vitamin A 0%	•	Vitamin C 4%
Calcium 3%	•	Iron 14%

Nutrition Grade D

* Based on a 2000 calorie diet

Ingredients
- 4-6 pounds grass-fed beef short ribs
- 1 lime, juiced
- 3 tablespoons Coconut Aminos
- 2 tablespoons apple cider vinegar
- 1 tablespoon raw honey
- 1 tablespoon olive oil
- 2 teaspoons grated fresh ginger
- 1 teaspoon red pepper sauce
- 1/4 teaspoon sea salt
- 1/4 teaspoon black pepper
- 1 small onion, chopped

- 3 cloves garlic, chopped
- 1 tablespoon Paleo Worcestershire sauce (see Recipe No. 62)

Directions
- To make the marinade, combine all ingredients except for the ribs in a small bowl; mix well. Place ribs in a shallow dish.
- Pour marinade over ribs and turn sides to coat. Cover and refrigerate for at least 8 hours.
- Transfer ribs into a 6-quart slow cooker and pour marinade over ribs. Cover the slow cooker and set to Low.
- Cook ribs for 6-8 hours or until tender.

45. Crock Pot Brazilian Chicken Curry

Servings: 6-8
Serving size: 1 medium bowl
Preparation time: 15 minutes
Cook time: 4-5 hours on HIGH, or 6-8 hours on LOW
Ready in: 4 hours and 15 minutes

Nutrition Facts

Serving Size 189 g

Amount Per Serving

Calories 226	Calories from Fat 88

	% Daily Value*
Total Fat 9.8g	**15%**
Saturated Fat 4.3g	**22%**
Trans Fat 0.0g	
Cholesterol 76mg	**25%**
Sodium 307mg	**13%**
Total Carbohydrates 7.7g	**3%**
Dietary Fiber 2.7g	**11%**
Sugars 2.8g	
Protein 26.1g	

Vitamin A 22%	•	Vitamin C 69%
Calcium 3%	•	Iron 17%

Nutrition Grade B+
* Based on a 2000 calorie diet

Ingredients
- 1.5-2 pounds chicken breasts
- 3/4 cup full-fat coconut milk (see Recipe No. 63)

- 2 tablespoons organic tomato paste (recommended: Tropical Traditions)
- 1 tablespoon fresh ginger, grated
- 3 cloves garlic, minced
- 4 tablespoons curry powder
- 1/2 teaspoon sea salt
- 1/4 teaspoon freshly ground black pepper
- 1 yellow bell pepper, diced
- 1 red bell pepper, diced
- 1 yellow onion, thinly sliced
- 1 cup pure chicken broth
- 1/2 cup organic coconut flakes (garnish)
- 3 tablespoons fresh cilantro, chopped (garnish)

Directions

- Rub chicken breasts with curry powder and place into a large bowl. Set aside.
- In a medium bowl, whisk together the coconut milk, tomato paste, ginger, garlic, sea salt and pepper. Stir in bell peppers and onion.
- Place chicken breasts in a 6-quart slow cooker. Pour the prepared coconut milk mixture over the chicken, and then add the chicken broth.
- Cover the slow cooker and cook chicken for 4-5 hours on High, or 6-8 hours on Low. Serve topped with coconut flakes and cilantro.

46. Honey Ginger Shredded Pork

Servings: 6-8
Preparation time: 15 minutes
Cook time: 6-8 hours on HIGH, or 8-10 hours on LOW
Ready in: 6 hours 15 minutes

Nutrition Facts

Serving Size 147 g

Amount Per Serving

Calories 261   Calories from Fat 101

	% Daily Value*
Total Fat 11.2g	**17%**
Saturated Fat 4.0g	**20%**
Trans Fat 0.0g	
Cholesterol 92mg	**31%**
Sodium 355mg	**15%**
Total Carbohydrates 5.4g	**2%**
Dietary Fiber 0.8g	**3%**
Sugars 2.9g	
Protein 33.0g	

Vitamin A 2%	•	Vitamin C 4%
Calcium 3%	•	Iron 11%

Nutrition Grade B

* Based on a 2000 calorie diet

Ingredients

- 2 pounds pork shoulder roast (or pork loin)
- 1 yellow onion, sliced
- 1/2 cup pure chicken broth
- 1 bay leaf

Spice mixture:

- 2 tablespoons freshly grated ginger
- 2 garlic cloves, peeled and crushed
- 2 teaspoons ground cumin
- 2 teaspoons ground coriander
- 1/2 teaspoon pepper
- 1/2 teaspoon smoked paprika
- 1 teaspoon cinnamon
- 1 teaspoon sea salt
- 1 tablespoon raw honey

Directions

- Combine all the ingredients for the spice mixture in a small bowl. Rub the prepared spice mixture all over the pork, and then place pork in a 4-quart slow cooker.
- Add the onion, bay leaf, and chicken broth.

- Cover the slow cooker and cook pork for 6-8 hours on High, or 8-10 hours on Low. Shred pork with tongs or 2 forks.

DESSERTS and SNACKS

47. Slow Cooked Maple Peach Applesauce

Servings: 8-10

Serving size: 3/4 cup

Preparation time: 15 minutes

Cook time: 3 hours on HIGH and 2 hours on LOW

Ready in: 5 hours and 15 minutes

Nutrition Facts

Serving Size 289 g

Amount Per Serving

Calories 156   Calories from Fat 1

	% Daily Value*
Total Fat 0.2g	**0%**
Trans Fat 0.0g	
Cholesterol 0mg	**0%**
Sodium 3mg	**0%**
Total Carbohydrates 40.9g	**14%**
Dietary Fiber 6.9g	**28%**
Sugars 31.1g	
Protein 0.5g	

Vitamin A 6%	Vitamin C 24%
Calcium 3%	Iron 3%

Nutrition Grade A

* Based on a 2000 calorie diet

Ingredients
- 10 Macintosh apples, peeled, cored and chopped
- 4 fresh peaches, peeled, pitted and chopped
- 1 tablespoon ground cinnamon
- 1 pinch unrefined brown sugar
- 2 tablespoons pure maple syrup
- 1/2 teaspoon fresh lemon juice
- 1/2 cup dried cranberries (optional)

Directions

- Place peaches and apples in a 4-quart slow cooker. Sprinkle the fruits with cinnamon and brown sugar, and then drizzle with maple syrup and lemon juice.
- Cover the slow cooker and cook fruits for 3 hours on High.
- Turn setting to Low, and then cook for another 2 hours. Stir in dried cranberries before serving.

48. Slow Cooked Pear-Cranberry Sauce

Servings: 4
Serving size: 1/2 cup
Preparation time: 5 minutes
Cook time: 2 hours on HIGH, or 4 hours on LOW.
Ready in: 2 hours and 5 minutes

Nutrition Facts

Serving Size 135 g

Amount Per Serving

Calories 177   Calories from Fat 2

% **Daily Value***

Total Fat 0.2g	**0%**
Trans Fat 0.0g	
Cholesterol 0mg	**0%**
Sodium 4mg	**0%**
Total Carbohydrates 47.7g	**16%**
Dietary Fiber 3.7g	**15%**
Sugars 40.3g	
Protein 0.7g	

Vitamin A 1%	Vitamin C 25%
Calcium 2%	Iron 3%

Nutrition Grade A
* Based on a 2000 calorie diet

Ingredients
- 1 3/4 cup fresh cranberries, rinsed
- 1 large pear, cored and diced
- 1 medium lemon, zested and juiced
- 1 tablespoon ginger, freshly grated
- 1 pinch cinnamon
- 1/2 cup raw honey (or pure maple syrup)

Directions

Combine thoroughly all the ingredients in a 4-quart slow cooker. Cook for 2 hours on High, or 4 hours on Low.

49. Crockpot Fig, Pear and Apple Butter

Servings: 9
Serving size: 1/2 cup
Preparation time: 10 minutes
Cook time: 6-8 hours on LOW
Ready in: 6 hours and 10 minutes

Nutrition Facts

Serving Size 274 g

Amount Per Serving

Calories 215	Calories from Fat 3

	% Daily Value*
Total Fat 0.4g	**1%**
Trans Fat 0.0g	
Cholesterol 0mg	**0%**
Sodium 33mg	**1%**
Total Carbohydrates 56.0g	**19%**
Dietary Fiber 8.2g	**33%**
Sugars 41.1g	
Protein 0.9g	

Vitamin A 2%	•	Vitamin C 17%
Calcium 7%	•	Iron 7%

Nutrition Grade A
* Based on a 2000 calorie diet

Ingredients

- 12 dried black figs, stems removed, cut in half
- 4 Bartlett pears, peeled, cored and diced
- 6 apples, peeled, cored and diced
- 1 cup apple cider
- 1/2 cup pure maple syrup
- 3 tablespoons ground cinnamon
- 1/4 teaspoon nutmeg
- 3 tablespoons ground ginger
- 1/2 teaspoon ground cloves
- 1 pinch of sea salt

Directions

- Combine all ingredients in a 4-quart slow cooker.
- Cover, and cook for 6-8 hours on Low until soft and almost mushy.
- Mash fruits until smooth and thick, or use a food processor to puree. Store in sealed jars and refrigerate.

50. Crock Pot Cranberry Pudding Cake

Servings: 6-8

Preparation time: 15 minutes

Cook time: 2 hours and 30 minutes on HIGH

Ready in: 2 hours and 45 minutes

Nutrition Facts

Serving Size 124 g

Amount Per Serving

Calories 186   Calories from Fat 123

	% Daily Value*
Total Fat 13.7g	**21%**
Saturated Fat 8.3g	**42%**
Trans Fat 0.0g	
Cholesterol 124mg	**41%**
Sodium 210mg	**9%**
Total Carbohydrates 11.6g	**4%**
Dietary Fiber 1.8g	**7%**
Sugars 7.1g	
Protein 6.1g	

Vitamin A 3%	•	Vitamin C 12%
Calcium 10%	•	Iron 8%

Nutrition Grade D+

* Based on a 2000 calorie diet

Ingredients
- 1 cup fresh cranberries
- 4 large eggs
- 1/4 cup fresh lemon juice
- 1/2 cup organic coconut cream concentrate, (recommended: Tropical Traditions), or see Recipe No. 62
- 1/2 cup full fat coconut milk (see Recipe No. 63)
- 2 tablespoons raw honey
- 1 teaspoon pure vanilla extract
- 1 cup almond flour
- 2 teaspoons baking powder

- 1/2 teaspoon sea salt
- Coconut oil cooking spray

Directions

- Coat the insert of a 5-quart slow cooker with cooking spray. Spread the cranberries over the bottom of the insert.
- In a large mixing bowl, beat the egg whites until frothy. Set aside.
- In another mixing bowl, whisk together the egg yolks, and then add the lemon juice, coconut cream, coconut milk, honey, and vanilla until well blended.
- Stir together the baking powder, almond flour, and sea salt in a medium bowl, and then add into the egg yolk mixture; continue beating until smooth. Fold egg yolk mixture into the egg whites.
- Pour batter over the cranberries in the slow cooker.
- Cover and cook for 2 hours and 30 minutes on High.

51. Crock Pot Caramel Poached Pears

Servings: 4
Serving size: 2 poached pear halves
Preparation time: 15 minutes
Cook time: 2 hours on HIGH
Ready in: 2 hours and 15 minutes

Nutrition Facts

Serving Size 313 g

Amount Per Serving

Calories 703   Calories from Fat 458

	% Daily Value*
Total Fat 50.8g	**78%**
Saturated Fat 36.8g	**184%**
Trans Fat 0.0g	
Cholesterol 0mg	**0%**
Sodium 11mg	**0%**
Total Carbohydrates 66.8g	**22%**
Dietary Fiber 8.7g	**35%**
Sugars 53.0g	
Protein 6.4g	

Vitamin A 0%	•	Vitamin C 14%
Calcium 4%	•	Iron 10%

Nutrition Grade C-

* Based on a 2000 calorie diet

Ingredients

- 1/2 cup coconut oil
- 1/2 cup raw honey
- 1 cup full-fat coconut milk (see Recipe No. 63)
- 1 tablespoon ginger, grated
- 4 firm and slightly ripe Bartlett pears, trimmed, peeled, halved lengthwise, and cored
- 1/8 teaspoon ground cinnamon
- 1/2 cup Toasted walnuts, chopped

Directions

- To make the caramel sauce, pour coconut oil and honey in a saucepan over medium heat, and bring to a boil until a caramel color is reached. Remove pan from heat, and then pour in the coconut milk. Blend well until smooth.
- Place the pears in a 4-quart slow cooker and sprinkle with grated ginger.
- Pour the prepared caramel sauce over pears; toss gently to coat.
- Cover the slow cooker and cook pears for 2 hours on High, or until fork tender. Transfer poached pears on serving plates. Top with caramel sauce and walnuts, then sprinkle with cinnamon.

52. Crock Pot Dark ChocNut Cups

Servings: 16

Serving size: 3 chocnut cups

Preparation time: 12 minutes

Cook time: 3 hours on LOW

Ready in: 3 hours and 12 minutes

Nutrition Facts

Serving Size 15 g

Amount Per Serving

Calories 72 — Calories from Fat 51

% Daily Value*

	% Daily Value*
Total Fat 5.7g	9%
Saturated Fat 0.7g	3%
Trans Fat 0.0g	
Cholesterol 0mg	0%
Sodium 12mg	0%
Total Carbohydrates 4.3g	1%
Dietary Fiber 0.7g	3%
Sugars 2.8g	
Protein 2.0g	

Vitamin A 0%	•	Vitamin C 0%
Calcium 1%	•	Iron 2%

Nutrition Grade B-

* Based on a 2000 calorie diet

Ingredients

- 1 cup walnuts, chopped (or almonds/hazelnuts)
- 2 cups semi-sweet chocolate chips
- 1 cup dark chocolate bars (more than 50% cocoa)
- 2 tablespoons unrefined brown sugar

Directions

- Line 2 (24-cup) mini muffin tins with mini muffin liners.
- Place chopped walnuts in the bottom of a 4-quart slow cooker. Add the semi-sweet chocolate chips and dark chocolate bars.
- Cook covered for 3 hours on Low. Spoon mixture onto lined muffin tins and let cool.

53. Crock Pot Candy-Coated Almonds

Servings: 10

Serving size: 1/2 – 3/4 cup

Preparation time: 10 minutes

Cook time: 3 hours on LOW

Ready in: 3 hours and 10 minutes

Nutrition Facts

Serving Size 81 g

Amount Per Serving

Calories 225   Calories from Fat 65

% **Daily Value***

Total Fat 7.2g	**11%**
Saturated Fat 1.9g	**9%**
Cholesterol 0mg	**0%**
Sodium 41mg	**2%**
Total Carbohydrates 39.6g	**13%**
Dietary Fiber 1.7g	**7%**
Sugars 36.4g	
Protein 2.7g	

Vitamin A 0%   •   Vitamin C 1%

Calcium 7%   •   Iron 9%

Nutrition Grade D

* Based on a 2000 calorie diet

Ingredients

- 1 egg white
- 2 teaspoons pure vanilla extract
- 3 1/2 cups whole raw almonds
- 3 tablespoon pumpkin pie spice
- 2 1/2 cup packed unrefined brown sugar
- 1/8 teaspoon sea salt
- 1/2 cup organic coconut flakes (recommended: Tropical Traditions)
- Coconut oil spray (for greasing)

Directions

- Whisk together the egg white and vanilla in a large bowl. Add the almonds and stir thoroughly to coat.
- Stir in the pumpkin pie spice, brown sugar, coconut flakes, and sea salt.
- Coat the insert of a 4-quart slow cooker with coconut oil spray. Place the coated almonds in the slow cooker and cook for 3 hours

on Low; stirring every 20 minutes until toasty. Allow to cool and store in an air-tight container.

54. Crock Pot Hot Choco

Servings: 6

Serving size: 1 cup

Preparation time: 2 hours and 30 minutes

Cook time: 2-3 hours on LOW

Ready in: 4 hours and 30 minutes

Nutrition Facts

Serving Size 341 g

Amount Per Serving

Calories 813	Calories from Fat 707

	% Daily Value*
Total Fat 78.6g	**121%**
Saturated Fat 68.3g	**342%**
Trans Fat 0.0g	
Cholesterol 0mg	**0%**
Sodium 79mg	**3%**
Total Carbohydrates 32.0g	**11%**
Dietary Fiber 7.4g	**29%**
Sugars 22.9g	
Protein 7.7g	

Vitamin A 0%	•	Vitamin C 15%
Calcium 5%	•	Iron 31%

Nutrition Grade D+

* Based on a 2000 calorie diet

Ingredients

- 2 cups coconut cream (see Recipe No. 62)
- 3 tablespoons raw honey
- 6 cups almond milk
- 2 cups semi-sweet chocolate chips, about 12 oz. (more than 50% cocoa)
- 1 teaspoon pure vanilla extract
- Pure peppermint extract (optional)

Directions

- Combine 1 3/4 cups coconut cream, almond milk, chocolate chips, and vanilla in a 4-quart slow cooker.
- Cover, and cook for 2-3 hours on Low. Blend well and ladle into mugs. Top with the remaining coconut cream and drizzle with pure peppermint extract.

55. Crock Pot Pina Colada Lava Cake

Servings: 6
Serving size: 1 medium bowl
Preparation time: 2 hours and 30 minutes
Cook time: 2-3 hours on HIGH, or 3-4 hours on LOW
Ready in: 4 hours and 30 minutes

Nutrition Facts

Serving Size 192 g

Amount Per Serving

Calories 338	Calories from Fat 274
	% Daily Value*
Total Fat 30.5g	47%
Saturated Fat 25.0g	125%
Cholesterol 0mg	0%
Sodium 18mg	1%
Total Carbohydrates 18.1g	6%
Dietary Fiber 4.5g	18%
Sugars 11.2g	
Protein 3.7g	

Vitamin A 1%	•	Vitamin C 65%
Calcium 9%	•	Iron 20%

Nutrition Grade C

* Based on a 2000 calorie diet

Ingredients

- 2 cups coconut cream (see Recipe No. 62)
- 1 (16 oz) can crushed pineapple, drained and juice reserved (recommended: Native Forest)
- 1 cup almond flour
- 1 1/2 teaspoon baking powder
- 1 teaspoon pure vanilla extract
- 2 tablespoon coconut oil
- 1 cup shredded coconut

Directions

- Spread drained pineapple into the bottom of a 4-quart slow cooker.
- Combine almond flour, baking powder, vanilla, coconut oil, 1/2 cup shredded coconut, 1/3 cup coconut cream, 2/3 cup of reserved pineapple juice, in a medium bowl. Stir thoroughly to incorporate. Spread batter on top of the pineapple.
- Combine 1 cup coconut milk and the remaining cream of coconut and bring to a boil. Pour boiling liquid mixture on top of the batter.
- Cover and cook for 2-3 hours on High, or for 3-4 hours on Low. Serve cake topped with shredded coconut.

56. Berry Banana Rhubarb Crisp

Servings: 6
Serving size: 1 medium plate/bowl
Preparation time: 15 minutes
Cook time: 2-3 hours on LOW
Ready in: 2 hours and 15 minutes

Nutrition Facts

Serving Size 212 g

Amount Per Serving

Calories 312   Calories from Fat 152

	% Daily Value*
Total Fat 16.9g	**26%**
Saturated Fat 6.9g	**35%**
Trans Fat 0.0g	
Cholesterol 0mg	**0%**
Sodium 48mg	**2%**
Total Carbohydrates 40.4g	**13%**
Dietary Fiber 5.3g	**21%**
Sugars 29.4g	
Protein 3.7g	

Vitamin A 2%	•	Vitamin C 58%
Calcium 9%	•	Iron 7%

Nutrition Grade B-

* Based on a 2000 calorie diet

Ingredients

- 2 cups diced rhubarb, cut into 1/2-inch pieces
- 1 1/2 cups diced strawberries
- 1 1/2 cups blueberries
- 1 cup banana, cut into 1-inch chunks
- 1/2 cup pure maple syrup
- 2 tablespoon lemon juice
- 1 teaspoon ground cinnamon
- 1/2 teaspoon ground nutmeg
- 1 cup almond flour
- 1 pinch sea salt
- 1/2 teaspoon ground nutmeg
- 2 tablespoon coconut oil
- 2 tablespoon maple syrup
- 1/2 cup pecans
- 2 tablespoon flax seeds
- 1 tablespoon coconut oil (for greasing)

Directions

- Lightly grease the inside of a 4-quart slow cooker with tablespoon coconut oil. Place the fruits in the slow cooker.

- Stir together the maple syrup, lemon juice, cinnamon, and nutmeg in a small bowl and pour mixture over fruits; gently toss to coat. Combine the remaining ingredients in another bowl, and then spread over the top of the fruit mixture.
- Cook for 2-3 hours on Low. Leave the lid slightly cracked in the last 30 minutes to allow excess liquid to evaporate. Place dessert in plates and serve.

57. Crock Pot Chocolate-Walnut Lava Cake

Servings: 8
Preparation time: 15 minutes
Cook time: 1-2 hours on HIGH
Ready in: 1 hour and 15 minutes

Nutrition Facts

Serving Size 189 g

Amount Per Serving	
Calories 507	Calories from Fat 304
	% Daily Value*
Total Fat 33.8g	**52%**
Saturated Fat 8.5g	**43%**
Cholesterol 35mg	**12%**
Sodium 20mg	**1%**
Total Carbohydrates 48.2g	**16%**
Dietary Fiber 5.5g	**22%**
Sugars 36.2g	
Protein 12.6g	

Vitamin A 1%	•	Vitamin C 1%
Calcium 19%	•	Iron 19%

Nutrition Grade C-
* Based on a 2000 calorie diet

Ingredients
- 1 1/2 cups almond flour
- 2 teaspoons baking powder
- 6 tablespoons almond butter
- 1/3 cup dark chocolate chips (more than 50% cocoa)
- 1 1/3 cup unrefined brown sugar
- 1/2 cup unsweetened cocoa powder
- 1 tablespoon pure vanilla extract
- 1/3 cup almond milk

- 1 egg yolk, organic is best
- 1 1/2 cups hot water
- 1 cup chopped walnuts
- 1 tablespoon coconut oil for greasing

Directions

- Coat the inside of a 3-quart slow cooker with coconut oil. In a medium bowl, whisk together the almond flour, 1/3 cup cocoa powder, and baking powder. Set aside.
- Place the chocolate chips and almond butter in a saucepan and melt over medium heat; stir to incorporate.
- Transfer melted chocolate mixture into a large mixing bowl. Add almond milk, egg yolk, 3 tablespoons cocoa, vanilla extract, and brown sugar. Stir in the flour mixture and chopped walnuts; blend well. Pour the batter into the slow cooker.
- Cover, and cook for 1-2 hours on High, or until set. Allow to cool and serve.

58. Choco-Apple Pot de Crème

Servings: 4
Serving size: 1 small ramekin or bowl
Preparation time: 15 minutes
Cook time: 8 hours on HIGH and 14 hours on LOW
Ready in: 22 hours and 15 minutes

Nutrition Facts

Serving Size 181 g

Amount Per Serving

Calories 256	Calories from Fat 114

	% Daily Value*
Total Fat 12.6g	**19%**
Saturated Fat 9.2g	**46%**
Trans Fat 0.0g	
Cholesterol 0mg	**0%**
Sodium 9mg	**0%**
Total Carbohydrates 39.3g	**13%**
Dietary Fiber 4.6g	**19%**
Sugars 31.1g	
Protein 2.2g	

Vitamin A 1%	•	Vitamin C 11%
Calcium 2%	•	Iron 7%

Nutrition Grade C

* Based on a 2000 calorie diet

Ingredients

- 1 pound Golden Delicious apples - peeled, cored and sliced
- 2 teaspoons apple cider vinegar
- 1/4 teaspoon ground cinnamon
- 1/8 teaspoon ground nutmeg
- 1/8 teaspoon ground cloves
- 1/4 cup and 2 1/2 tablespoons unrefined brown sugar
- 1 cup ripe avocado flesh
- 1 tablespoon cocoa powder
- 1/2 cup almond milk
- 1 teaspoon raw honey
- 1/2 dark chocolate chips (to garnish)

Directions

- Place apples and cider vinegar into a 4-quart slow cooker.
- Cover, and cook for 8 hours on High. Set slow cooker to Low, and cook 10 hours more. Stir in cinnamon, nutmeg, cloves, and brown sugar; cook 4 hours more. Spoon apple butter into small ramekins or bowls.
- Combine avocado, cocoa powder, almond milk, and honey in a blender, and blend until smooth.

- Spoon crème over apple butter in ramekins. Sprinkle chocolate chips on top and serve.

59. Crockpot Baked Orange Custard

Servings: 4
Serving size: 1 cup
Preparation time: 15 minutes
Cook time: 2.5-3 hours on HIGH
Ready in: 2 hours and 45 minutes

Nutrition Facts

Serving Size 184 g

Amount Per Serving

Calories 422   Calories from Fat 294

	% Daily Value*
Total Fat 32.7g	**50%**
Saturated Fat 26.5g	**133%**
Trans Fat 0.0g	
Cholesterol 123mg	**41%**
Sodium 65mg	**3%**
Total Carbohydrates 30.8g	**10%**
Dietary Fiber 2.9g	**12%**
Sugars 27.6g	
Protein 7.3g	

Vitamin A 3%	•	Vitamin C 7%
Calcium 4%	•	Iron 15%

Nutrition Grade D+

* Based on a 2000 calorie diet

Ingredients
- 3 eggs, lightly beaten
- 2 cups almond milk
- 1/3 cup raw honey
- 1 teaspoon pure vanilla extract
- 1/4 teaspoon ground cinnamon
- 1/4 teaspoon ground nutmeg
- 3/4 teaspoon orange peel, finely shredded
- 1 teaspoon almond butter (for greasing)

Directions

- In a mixing bowl, whisk together the eggs, almond milk, honey, orange peel, and vanilla. Lightly grease a 1- or 1 1/2-quart soufflé dish with almond butter.
- Pour egg mixture into the soufflé dish, and sprinkle cinnamon and nutmeg. Place a wire rack in a 4-quart slow cooker, and then pour hot water into the cooker around the dish, about 1 1/2 inches deep.
- Cover the soufflé dish with aluminum foil and place on top of the wire rack in the slow cooker.
- Cover the slow cooker and cook for 2 1/2 to 3 hours on high.

60. Crock Pot Stewed Apples

Servings: 4
Preparation time: 10 minutes
Cook time: 4 hours on LOW
Ready in: 4 hours and 10 minutes

Nutrition Facts

Serving Size 397 g

Amount Per Serving

Calories 532   Calories from Fat 64

	% Daily Value*
Total Fat 7.1g	**11%**
Saturated Fat 0.7g	**4%**
Trans Fat 0.0g	
Cholesterol 0mg	**0%**
Sodium 14mg	**1%**
Total Carbohydrates 120.6g	**40%**
Dietary Fiber 12.0g	**48%**
Sugars 86.1g	
Protein 4.1g	

Vitamin A 12%	•	Vitamin C 22%
Calcium 11%	•	Iron 9%

Nutrition Grade B

* Based on a 2000 calorie diet

Ingredients
- 2 pounds tart apples, sliced cored, and peeled
- 1/2 pound prunes
- 1/2 pound dried pears
- 1 teaspoon cinnamon
- 1 dash ground nutmeg

- 3 tablespoons arrowroot powder
- 1 teaspoon pure vanilla extract
- 1 cup unrefined brown sugar
- 3 tablespoons almond butter, diced

Directions

Combine all the ingredients in a 4-quart slow cooker; toss to coat. Cook for 4 hours on Low. Stir once after 1 hour. Serve warm.

CONDIMENTS

61. Ketchup

Yield: 1 1/2 cups
Preparation time: 5 minutes
Cook time: 15 minutes
Ready in: 20 minutes

Nutrition Facts

Serving Size 85 g

Amount Per Serving

Calories 71	Calories from Fat 1
	% Daily Value*
Total Fat 0.1g	0%
Trans Fat 0.0g	
Cholesterol 0mg	0%
Sodium 200mg	8%
Total Carbohydrates 17.0g	6%
Dietary Fiber 2.2g	9%
Sugars 15.3g	
Protein 1.6g	

| Vitamin A 13% | • | Vitamin C 14% |
| Calcium 3% | • | Iron 6% |

Nutrition Grade B-

* Based on a 2000 calorie diet

Ingredients
- 1 1/2 cups crushed tomatoes, drained and pressed
- 1/4 cup raw honey
- 3 tablespoon lemon juice
- 1/4 teaspoon dry mustard
- 1/4 teaspoon sea salt

- 1/4 teaspoon ground cloves
- 1/4 teaspoon ground cinnamon
- 1/8 teaspoon cayenne pepper

Directions

- Put all ingredients in a blender and blend well until creamy.
- Transfer the mixture into a saucepan and bring to a boil over medium heat. Simmer for 15 minutes; stirring occasionally.
- Allow to cool, then pour ketchup into a jar and refrigerate.

62. Worcestershire sauce

Yield: 1 cup
Preparation time: 8 minutes
Cook time: 20 minutes
Ready in: 28 minutes

Nutrition Facts

Serving Size 353 g

Amount Per Serving

Calories 46   Calories from Fat 3

	% Daily Value*
Total Fat 0.3g	0%
Trans Fat 0.0g	
Cholesterol 0mg	0%
Sodium 234mg	10%
Total Carbohydrates 5.1g	2%
Dietary Fiber 0.5g	2%
Sugars 1.0g	
Protein 0.5g	

Vitamin A 0%	•	Vitamin C 1%
Calcium 2%	•	Iron 3%

Nutrition Grade B-
* Based on a 2000 calorie diet

Ingredients

- 1/2 cup apple cider vinegar
- 2 tablespoon water
- 2 tablespoon Coconut Aminos
- 1/4 teaspoon onion powder
- 1/4 teaspoon ground ginger

- 1/8 teaspoon cinnamon
- 1/4 teaspoon mustard powder
- 1/4 teaspoon garlic powder
- 1/8 teaspoon freshly ground black pepper

Directions
- Mix all the ingredients in a blender and blend until smooth.
- Transfer mixture into a saucepan and bring to a boil over medium heat. Reduce heat to medium-low and cook for about 15 minutes; stirring frequently, or until sauce is thick.
- Cool, store in a sealed jar, and refrigerate.

63. Coconut milk

Yield: 4 cups
Preparation time: 10 minutes
Ready in: 10 minutes

Nutrition Facts

Serving Size 1068 g

Amount Per Serving

Calories 560 — Calories from Fat 432

	% Daily Value*
Total Fat 48.0g	**74%**
Saturated Fat 40.0g	**200%**
Trans Fat 0.0g	
Cholesterol 0mg	**0%**
Sodium 28mg	**1%**
Total Carbohydrates 32.0g	**11%**
Dietary Fiber 16.0g	**64%**
Protein 8.0g	

Vitamin A 0%	•	Vitamin C 0%
Calcium 3%	•	Iron 0%

Nutrition Grade C-
* Based on a 2000 calorie diet

Ingredients
- 2 cups organic unsweetened shredded coconut
- 4 cups hot water

Directions
Full-fat Coconut Milk:

- Combine the shredded coconut and water in a blender.
- Blend on high for at least 1 minute until smooth. Allow to cool for 5 minutes.
- Pour coconut mixture into a strainer through a cheese cloth and press cheesecloth into a jar or pitcher.

Light Coconut Milk: (second pressing)

- Place the dry-pressed coconut pulp back into the blender. Add 1 1/2 cup of hot water and blend at high speed for 2 minutes.
- Strain and press the milk out of the pulp again into a jar or pitcher.

Allow to cool, and then refrigerate. Use within 3-4 days for best flavor and texture.

64. Barbecue sauce

Yield: 2 cups
Preparation time: 5 minutes
Cook time: 35 minutes
Ready in: 40 minutes

Nutrition Facts

Serving Size 762 g

Amount Per Serving

Calories 499   Calories from Fat 140

% Daily Value*

Total Fat 15.6g	**24%**
Saturated Fat 1.4g	**7%**
Trans Fat 0.0g	
Cholesterol 0mg	**0%**
Sodium 1367mg	**57%**
Total Carbohydrates 77.6g	**26%**
Dietary Fiber 15.7g	**63%**
Sugars 45.0g	
Protein 19.3g	

Vitamin A 72%	•	Vitamin C 127%
Calcium 28%	•	Iron 55%

Nutrition Grade A

* Based on a 2000 calorie diet

Ingredients

- 1 teaspoon olive oil
- 1 onion, minced
- 1 clove garlic, minced

- 1 tablespoon Coconut Aminos
- 3/4 cup tomato paste
- 1/2 cup apple cider vinegar
- 1/4 cup organic paleo ketchup, (see Recipe No. 61)
- 3 tablespoon mustard
- 1 pinch ground cloves
- 1 tablespoon hot sauce
- 1 pinch cinnamon
- 1/2 cup water

Directions

- Sauté onion in olive oil over medium heat, until golden brown. Add garlic and cook for another minute.
- Stir in the remaining ingredients and simmer for 30 minutes.
- Store in a sealed jar and refrigerate.

65. Coconut Cream

Yield: 2 cups
Preparation time: 2 hours and 25 minutes
Ready in: 2 hours and 25 minutes

Nutrition Facts

Serving Size 379 g

Amount Per Serving

Calories 392   Calories from Fat 162

	% Daily Value*
Total Fat 18.0g	28%
Saturated Fat 16.0g	80%
Trans Fat 0.0g	
Cholesterol 0mg	0%
Sodium 23mg	1%
Total Carbohydrates 55.9g	19%
Sugars 51.7g	
Protein 0.2g	

Vitamin A 0%	•	Vitamin C 1%
Calcium 0%	•	Iron 1%

Nutrition Grade D-
* Based on a 2000 calorie diet

Ingredients

- 4 cups full-fat coconut milk (see Recipe No. 63), or organic, gum-free and BPA-free coconut milk
- 3 tablespoons raw honey

Directions
- Refrigerate coconut milk in a sealed container for at least 2 hours, overnight is best. Chill a mixing bowl and a hand mixer or beater in the freezer for at least 5-10 minutes.
- Remove coconut cream from the fridge. Transfer the solidified cream that has risen to the top into the pre-chilled mixing bowl; discard the thinner coconut water underneath.
- Beat the coconut cream until thick. Stir in honey and refrigerate for 15 minutes.

Books by Andrea Huffington

Paleo Slow Cooker Recipes

Going Paleo on a Budget

www.amazon.com/author/andrea-huffington

About Andrea Huffington

Andrea Huffington is an author, professional speaker and health coach extraordinaire.

Growing up in Southern California, Andrea has struggled with being overweight since early childhood. After completing a degree in chemical engineering at UCLA (where she also met her husband James), she took an internship in India. Shortly thereafter she had to return to the United States to receive treatment for her progressively worsening diabetes. After this health scare and trying various different diets and approaches, she found the Paleo way of eating and has never looked back. Today she is a picture of health and wellness, and participates in triathlons and frequently gives talks on the subject of how the Paleo diet impacts sports fitness and emotional health.

She believes that in keeping things simple we can achieve so much more. This has certainly worked for her!

Recently Andrea has spent three months with the San people of the Kalahari Desert in a quest to discover the secrets of their endurance and stamina in hot desert conditions.

Andrea lives in Hawaii with her husband, three children, two dogs and a pet Boa Constrictor.

One Last Thing...

Thank you so much for reading my book. I hope you really liked it. As you probably know, many people look at the reviews on Amazon before they decide to purchase a book. If you liked the book, could you please take a minute to leave a review with your feedback? 60 seconds is all I'm asking for, and it would mean the world to me.

Andrea Huffington

Primal Publishing

Atlanta, Georgia USA

Made in the USA
Lexington, KY
02 September 2013